THE MAN BEHIND THE MIRACLE

MADELINE HARTMANN

LOST
COAST
Fort Bragg
California

The Man Behind the Miracle
Copyright © 2000 Madeline Hartmann

Lost Coast Press
155 Cypress Street
Fort Bragg, CA 95437
1-800-773-7782

Publisher's Cataloging-in-Publication
(Provided by Quality Books, Inc.)

Hartmann, Madeline.
    The man behind the miracle : the story of
Alfred Boeddeker / Madeline Hartmann
    p. cm.
    LCCN: 99-076569
    ISBN: 1-882897-40-4

    1. Boeddeker, Alfred. 2. Priests--California--
San Francisco--Biography. 3. Franciscans--
Biography. 4. San Francisco (Calif.)--Biography.
5. Soup kitchens--California--San Francisco.
1.Title

BX4075.B64H37 2000   271'302 [B]
                        QBI99-1732

Cover painting by Eugenia Gogalowska

Printed in the United States of America

Dedicated to Father's many guests

and the people who made it all possible.

Madeline Hartman

ACKNOWLEDGMENTS

- Frank and Teresa Boeddeker, for hours of interviews plus many more hours of informal discussion.
- Father Giles Valcovich, OFM, for his help and great moral support.
- Beth Payne, Father Alfred's secretary and an archive of information.
- Sister Sheila Keane, OP, for her wonderful stories.
- Marie and John Richard, for encouragement when it seemed as if the whole project would not even get started.
- Joan McCarthy, for listening to me and then saying, "Did you know that?" No, I didn't.
- Pat McShane, who was very supportive.
- Paul J. McCarthy, who had details no one else could possibly have had.
- Father Floyd Lotito, OFM for his insights on nearly 30 years of close association with Father Alfred.
- Father John Vaughn, OFM, former minister general of the Franciscans, for clearing up many questions.
- Dr. Francis Curry, a long-time close associate of Alfred, who despite his frailties, gave me a great deal of time.
- Frank and Greta Schepergerdes, for long in-depth interviews about thirty-five years with Alfred.
- Gene Benedetti, a great source of information about the St. Anthony Farm.
- Richard Geiger of the *San Francisco Chronicle* for his help with the archive.

ADDITIONAL ACKNOWLEDGMENTS

- Dr. Hejo Boeddeker of Essen, Germany.
- Dr. William Doyle, Knight Commander of the Knights of the Holy Sepulcher.
- Rev. Mother Armida Andrade of Casa de los Pobres.
- The Honorable George Christopher, former mayor of San Francisco.
- Frank Clark of La Madre de los Pobres.
- Ron Stringham, who saved the whole thing.
- Paul Tapia, for his graphical expertise.
- Vicki Hessel Werkley, editor *par excellence*.
- Father Finian McGinn, OFM, Minister Provincial of Santa Barbara

and

- Sister Patrick Curran, RSM of the St. Anthony Foundation. For your faith and vision, thanks.

Apologies to whomever I left out. It was not intentional.
A work such as this needs many voices.

FOREWORD

I am so pleased to be able to recognize and pay tribute to the good work and lifetime achievements of Father Alfred Boeddeker. Simply put, he was one of the most kind and devoted persons I have ever known, and I had the great fortune to call him a friend.

When one lives such a full and compassionate life, such as Father Boeddeker, he touches the lives of many. His life was spent in service to others, and he was a testament to the human spirit that we would all like to see within ourselves.

I am especially proud that Father Boeddeker called San Francisco home, and was one of its native sons. Although his service to the Church took him on travels throughout the world, San Francisco was one of the primary benefactors of his dedicated service and good deeds.

For over 40 years he served his fellow San Franciscans as Pastor of St. Boniface Church. When Father Boeddeker established St. Anthony Dining Room in 1950, it was one of the first of its kind in the nation. Hoping to reinforce the highest possible dignity in those whom he served, he abolished the bread lines and established a warm, safe place where the needy and poor could receive a balanced meal every weekday of the year at no charge or obligation. As Father Boeddeker was constantly trying to bring people together, both the guests and helpers of the

Dining Room represent diverse backgrounds as to race, religion and other differences.

As in most places where you would find Father Boeddeker, St. Anthony Dining Room was a special place to be, and I spent many afternoons helping to serve meals there. I was always touched by his grace and benevolence. He was concerned and responsive to everyone's needs, and each individual felt important and loved in his presence. Perhaps this was his greatest achievement of all.

I can think of few people that I respected, admired and acclaimed more than Father Boeddeker. He was a gift to San Francisco and to humanity.

—Dianne Feinstein, United States Senator and former mayor of San Francisco.

Thousands of admirers and grateful beneficiaries of our late beloved Alfred Boeddeker to this day mention his name with total reverence and gratitude that he lived in our midst.

During my eight years as mayor of San Fransicco, I frequently walked to his nearby chapel to speak with him, and each time I left with a replenished spirit and confidence in the goodness of humankind, for Father Boeddeker himself was a human, living Angel on earth, the embodiment of spiritual inspiration—a true Apostle of charity and goodness.

He was a morale builder to the afflicited, to the desolate, the ill and forgotten souls who sought his counsel, and were the beneficiaries of his charitable heart. He embraced them all with loving care.

I am grateful that a Gracious Benevolent God allowed me to live in an era when a living Angel—Father Boeddeker was at my side and gave me the benefit of his inspiration and counsel on behalf of the people of San Francisco.

—George Christopher, mayor 1956-1964

AUTHOR'S NOTE

Father Alfred Boeddeker, my beloved cousin and good friend, was laid to rest on January 3, 1994. From the moment I got into my car for the three-hour drive to his funeral, all during the Mass and the reception that followed, I heard a voice inside my head saying, "Father deserves a biography. Father deserves a book. But I'm sure I'm not the person to write it." However, a year and a half later, I began conducting interviews with people who knew, loved and worked with Alfred. This book demanded to be written. It is an anecdotal biography based on those interviews plus a great deal of written material. Perhaps one day a scholarly work will be written based on the wealth of his spiritual and theological writings and notes, now stored in the Santa Barbara Mission archives. That was not the thrust of this book.

INTRODUCTION

Mama, if I don't become a Franciscan, I don't know what I will do with my life."

That was Anton "Tony" Boeddeker at the age of eleven begging to be allowed to enter the Franciscan Seminary at Santa Barbara, California.

"Father, if you hadn't become a Franciscan, you would be the CEO and Chairman of the Board of the world's largest multinational conglomerate."

That was Marvin Cardoza, a prominent businessman and good friend, acting as toastmaster of the 80th birthday celebration for Father Alfred Boeddeker, Order of Friars Minor, at a Fairmont Hotel luncheon, San Francisco, California in 1983.

Yes, he did become a Franciscan. Yes, indeed! He became one of those friars who followed the rule of St. Francis. It had been a long life's journey for the son of German immigrants to that civic reception with telegrams of congratulation from the President of the United States, the Governor of California, Senators and Representatives, with notables, friends, family and supporters in attendance.

There were long years of study and training at the St. Anthony Seminary of the Old Mission, Santa Barbara, followed by ordination at the age of twenty-three. There were the three years of study in Rome for a doctorate in Canon Law. There were extensive travels in Europe and the Holy

Land during his vacations in the turbulent 1930s and a return to Santa Barbara to teach theology, canon law, and sacred liturgy at his alma mater. At the same time, he served as canon lawyer to the bishop of San Diego, California. And in his spare time he established a social center for African-American and Hispanic children in the underprivileged area of affluent Santa Barbara.

In the late 1940s there were further studies in Asian Affairs at the University of California, Berkeley to prepare for missionary work in China. The Franciscan Friars wished to establish a university in Hankow, and Alfred joyously asked for the assignment. For him there could be no greater calling than to be a Franciscan missionary. These plans were cancelled in 1949 when China, under its new leaders, closed its doors to the West expelling, jailing or executing Westerners—missionaries in particular.

Alfred, age forty-seven, was without a job. One career was behind him, and another—eagerly anticipated—was in shambles. If he was disappointed, he gave no sign. He quietly continued to do parish work at St. Elizabeth's Church in Oakland where he had been living. He put his trust in his God and accepted His will.

At his mother's funeral in August 1949, he told his assembled family that he had been appointed pastor of St. Boniface Church in San Francisco. "Pastor of our German church" was the delighted response. Established in the 1860s, St. Boniface, a Franciscan church named for the patron saint of Germany, was the spiritual and cultural center of the German-American Catholic community of the San Francisco Bay Area and Northern California. Many German immigrants and their offspring had been married at this church, including Alfred's parents. Many of the children, Alfred for one, had been baptized there. His brother Joe and others in the family had been altar boys, had attended St. Boniface School, had gone to church there. All had taken part in the life of the parish.

What the family did not realize—and Alfred was too humble and obedient to say—was that St. Boniface was not exactly an upward career move: from theology professor, canon lawyer, designated university founder and president ...to pastor of a poor, inner city parish in San Francisco's Tenderloin—an area noted for its Skid Row, burlesque theaters, sleazy bars, honky-tonk night life, prostitution, hustling and crime. The buildings in the area were generally rundown; the streets dirty and greasy. And the smell of the Tenderloin was very powerful and distinctive: urine. People living in what some have called Dante's Inferno were very poor, many of them old, crammed in residential hotels or tiny apartments. The folk wisdom in San Francisco was that the Tenderloin was a place to avoid. "Don't walk through there if you don't have to." Society seemed to have stashed its untouchables there ...the lepers of our modern society.

No, St. Boniface was not a great assignment, but Alfred was pleased. No one could guess that two very powerful forces would now meet: Father Alfred and the City of San Francisco. Out of that encounter would come remarkable things.

St. Boniface had as its parishioners not only people from the Tenderloin, but also downtown workers and shoppers who attended Mass on their noon hour. Businessmen—such as the president of a well-known bank whose headquarters was just around the corner—and union members whose halls were across the street dropped into the church. Workers at City Hall a few blocks away visited on their breaks; people from Nob Hill, site of luxury homes and apartments and world-famous hotels such as the Fairmont and the Mark Hopkins also attended this church on occasion. All these would soon join Father Alfred in the greatest undertaking of his life.

From down-and-outers to movers-and-shakers of the City, here Alfred, nearly fifty, would begin his greatest work. Here he would find challenges which could daunt even a man of his vision, talent and dedication. The City of St. Francis had a Franciscan in its midst who cared deeply and passionately about the poor, the sick, the homeless, the hungry, the unloved and the forgotten. Caring would be translated into action. Alfred accomplished things many regarded as impossible. Gathering supporters from all segments of the City, he would help his poor with aid from powerful, wealthy people and average citizens too. He would ask for a "buck a month" from working people and get an outpouring of money. Father's voice would come out of the Tenderloin and be heard throughout the City. In time it would resonate far beyond San Francisco and California to be heard around the world.

Who was this man who would found the St. Anthony Dining Room and many, many other enterprises to help the poor and forgotten? "One of the good ones," a priest in Guatemala told a niece. Alfred was a man of great simplicity and great complexity, with a simple faith steeped in profound theology. A follower of St. Francis, he wore the brown robe of the Franciscans with great joy and had what the British writer G.K. Chesterton called the spirit of that saint: "A reckless faith not only in God but in man."

FAMILY

*The great activity of our life is to love. I see God as
one act—just loving—like the sun always shining.*
—Alfred

The Boeddeker family—part of the last century's great
tide of European immigration, which helped define
much of the American character—came from a tiny village in Westphalia, Germany. Alhausen was not even
on the map . . . "it is over the hill from Bad Driburg—
just go a little way and you are there."

San Francisco, halfway around the world, was a long
journey. Henry and Ferdinand Gelhaus, Alfred's uncles,
settled in Marysville, California in the 1880s. They asked
their sister, Bertha, to join them, hoping such distance
would encourage her to forget the poor orphan the rest
of the family regarded as totally unsuitable for her. Perhaps she just might marry a fellow immigrant from the
same town, now a very wealthy landowner with 5000
acres of rich river bottomland producing grain. Wheat
was then the principal crop of the Central Valley.

Bertha and her 16-year-old niece, Louise, made the
long journey by ship and train to California. Bertha met
the people of Marysville and the wealthy landowner,
but her heart was spoken for. She saw a new land with
new opportunities and—just maybe—less class pre-
judice against an orphan. She wrote to her father in

1

Germany, telling him she did not think she would return to Europe: the ocean voyage had made her sick! She moved to San Francisco and found employment as a cook in the home of a wealthy Jewish family.

Every morning at six, Bertha and the Irish maid upstairs walked to St. Boniface Church to hear Mass. Carefully she saved her money and after seven years, had a tidy nest egg. She sent to her beloved Joseph Boeddeker—now a master carpenter—the passage money to join her. Traditions were strict even for a woman who had shown as much independence as Bertha. Joe went to her father and on bended knee asked Gelhaus's permission and blessings to marry the daughter in faraway California.

Joseph already had a tie to America. When he was fourteen his parents died. Shortly thereafter, his elder brother went to the United States and was never heard from again. Joe tried for many years to find him but without success.

The name Boeddeker is quite unusual even in Germany. Its origins go back to the time of the Emperor Charlemagne around AD 800 and are rather colorful. A noble Saxon woman whose husband had died in the long wars between the Franks (Charlemagne) and the Saxons, fled to the court of Charlemagne to seek protection from the unwanted attentions of her brother-in-law. Her child, a son, was born perhaps on the way; tradition states under a linden tree. It is more likely that the child was born in the palace of the king at Paderborn. The baby was baptized in the cathedral there, the heart of Saxon territory, and the locale of much of the conflict. Charlemagne personally lifted the baby from the baptismal font, thereby signifying that he was the godfather and taking the responsibility to rear the boy.

Magenulf (in English; Meinulf in German) went to the cathedral school in Paderborn. After completion of his studies, he took orders and decided to start a convent for women on the spot where a certain deer came to drink. Tradition has it that the deer had a cross between its antlers. Nuns came to the convent from either France or the city of Aachen in Germany. The monastery became a religious center from which Magenulf preached to his Saxon compatriots. On his death in 857 he was buried in the local cemetery. Canonized not long afterward, he became known as one of the Apostles of Westphalia. The convent was called Boeddeken. The people of the village took the name as a family name. The "n" was changed to "r" to make it easier to pronounce, and it became Boeddeker. Variations to this include Boedekker and Boedikker, as well as others.

THE FAMILY GROWS

My saintly parents . . . " To the end of his life, Alfred praised his parents for their caring, their devotion, their training, their example and their influence.

The West was building. Joe, a highly skilled master carpenter, found employment quickly. The couple was married at St. Boniface Church, and Bertha's employers gave the wedding reception. Perhaps the latkes—the potato pancakes Bertha had learned to make—were served.

The couple settled in the South of Market area on Minna Street near St. Boniface Church. This was the high tide of European immigration, and each national group had its own church trying to maintain an ethnic identity in the turmoil and confusion of assimilation in the New World. Such churches in San Francisco included St. Peter and Paul's in North Beach for the Italians, St. Anthony's for the Sicilians, Notre Dame de Victoires for the small French colony, Our Lady of Guadeloupe for the Spanish-speaking people and St. Patrick's for the Irish. Old World religious and national holidays were celebrated. Sermons were preached in the respective languages and instruction in the parochial schools was bilingual—a comforting tie to a distant homeland. In the Old Country these diverse groups, languages and cultures had been names on a map to be learned in school. Now they were neighbors, fellow workers, the

4

children's playmates and sometimes even friends. In time, the immigrant children would intermarry, sometimes to the disapproval of the parents.

Bertha and Joseph's family began. First Joe, Jr.; then came Louise, Marie and Anne. Anton (later Alfred) was born on August 7, 1903. All were baptized at St. Boniface Church. Joseph worked hard to build a family home; in addition he constructed two houses, which the family hoped to sell. The Boeddekers would then be "well fixed." They planned to use a portion of the money to pay for a visit to the Old Country, then return to San Francisco and continue contracting houses. A bright and prosperous future beckoned.

Instead, disaster stuck. On April 18, 1906 the City was leveled by a powerful earthquake. The South of Market area, much of which had been part of San Francisco Bay, was filled land. The soil liquefied in the quake, and the houses collapsed like matchboxes. Homes, businesses and factories, which the immigrants had proudly built of brick to last a lifetime, were the worst hit. They fell, crushing people to death. This was followed by the fire. The Boeddeker family was given ten minutes to vacate their house before it was dynamited to stop the spread of the flames. They fled, but the dynamiting did not work. The fire burned much of the South of Market area and downtown. Everyone in the fire's path lost everything. Most of the people of the City were immigrants with their children, just getting a start in the New World. For San Francisco and its people—the Boeddekers among them—it was the nadir of their fortunes.

The Boeddeker family lost no family members, but they were financially ruined. They found refuge across the Bay at St. Elizabeth's Church, in the Fruitvale District of Oakland, which provided temporary sanctuary for many fire and quake victims. For one year the Boeddekers stayed with Bertha's niece, Louise Dombrink, and her family. Many who fled to Oakland, including the Boeddekers, decided to relocate out of San Francisco. There was a great fear that another earthquake would occur there. Better to stay in Oakland, which was safer. People did not know then about the Hayward Fault.

All this relocation created an urgent need for new housing—a building boom—so Joe's skills were in great demand. It was said he needed only to measure the first upright of a building, and then he could put everything else in place by dead reckoning—and be absolutely accurate. His skill and reputation made him a successful contractor who eventually built more than 100 houses in Oakland, mostly in the Fruitvale district.

The arrival of Teresa, Josephine and Frank completed the family. A large house was needed, and Joe worked on that in between building contract houses. Meanwhile, the family lived in a shed on property purchased on 34th Avenue. For the devout Boeddekers, the important thing was that it was only a few hundred yards from St. Elizabeth's. This Franciscan church, organized in 1893 by Germans in the area, became the spiritual, educational and social center of their lives.

While the house was being built, Anton (Tony) climbed where he should not; he fell and caught his lip on a nail, tearing it. Bertha put sauerkraut on the cut to stop the bleeding and to disinfect the wound. Naturally, a German household had a plentiful supply of sauerkraut. As a disinfectant it worked, but Alfred carried the scar all his life.

German remained the language of the home. The children grew up bilingual—which would stand Alfred in good stead all his life. All attended St. Elizabeth's School, and the sons were altar boys. The children acted as children: studying, playing as well as getting into mischief. Once Anne and Tony were playing soldiers in the backyard. He got one of his mother's cooking pots with side handles and put it on his head like a helmet. It was summer. It was hot. Tony started to sweat; his hair got soaked from the sweat; his face started to swell. But the pot would not come off. He started to scream. Finally the pot had to be cut off. Poor Bertha lost one of her good pots, which was tough on a tight budget.

The kids in the neighborhood played baseball with balls they made of rags. Baseball was Tony's best game. He was so good at the sport that his father had to buy a shoemaker's kit to repair the soles and heels of his shoes, which did not last a week. Sliding into bases was hard on shoes.

That childhood had other effects. Years later Alfred's staff had trouble reading his tiny handwriting and someone asked, "Father, how come you write so small?"

"When I was growing up we were very poor, so we saved paper! Paper was very expensive."

During school vacations, the older children would visit relatives who owned a farm in Petaluma, where they found animals, open space, a barn with a loft and hay. It was a marvelous place to play—or to sit and dream. Tony particularly liked to sit in the loft and dangle his feet over the edge. After watching him do this over several days, "Tante" announced that he was lazy and "would never amount to anything."

VOCATION

Throughout his long life, Alfred often spoke of his parents with love, respect and admiration. "We were a religious family—not superstitiously religious but solidly religious. It was part of life and consisted not only in prayer but in justice, in charity. There was a certain type of unselfishness that we were, I won't say drilled in, but encouraged to practice. It was an atmosphere you lived in, and I believe we had very good ideals . . . not beyond our reach, but there was a certain stimulus that was always to give."

By the age of eleven Tony had a strong religious calling, but he was also a great admirer of Marie, a young lady in his class. The priesthood won, and he remained friends with Marie and her husband all their lives. Years later Alfred told a niece, "I really liked Marie and had to think seriously if she was someone I wanted in my life or did I want the priesthood. I had to choose."

When he announced his intention to enter the seminary, his family was delighted but wished him to wait. They thought he was too young. Most entered at thirteen or fourteen; Tony was eleven. He had to fight his family and the Franciscans to be admitted at that age.

The school principal, Sister Rosario, O.P. (Dominicans), tried to persuade him to wait just one more year. He settled the matter by telling her she would be responsible for his missing a year of priesthood—all those Masses unsaid, good works not done. She decided to support so determined a young man and helped him overcome the opposition of his family and the Franciscans. In June 1914, Tony departed for Santa Barbara.

EDUCATION

As a child, I always saw the brown robe. To me, to be a priest was to one day wear this robe. Now I connect the priesthood and the Franciscan way of life, which is just another manifestation of the kind of love that I could see in Christ and St. Francis of Assisi.
—Alfred

Santa Barbara is a southern California city between mountains and sea with a mild climate, wonderful flora and great natural beauty. It is protected from cold winds of the Pacific by the Channel Islands. The mountains behind it hold back the heat of the Great Central Valley. Many consider it to be one of the loveliest cities in the United States.

It was founded in 1776 with the building of the Old Mission by Spanish Franciscan friars. Today Santa Barbara is still known as the Queen of the Missions and is the largest of all twenty-one California Spanish Missions.

Here in this serene setting began the long years of training necessary to be a Franciscan priest. Tony's life was now filled with studies, sports, his beloved baseball, prayer and discipline. He wrote home about the games that they played and who won. Often it was the Fruitvale Boys. This section of Oakland had so many seminarians that they could field a team. Father Terence, who was in the seminary with Tony, commented that he was a very fine athlete, outstanding in baseball and football, very good at basketball, soccer and tennis. "He was very well coordinated." Father Terence went on to comment that even in the seminary, Alfred's great charm, kindness and caring were evident. "He was very popular. A leader. An excellent scholar. A kind and gentle person. We all liked him and looked up to him."

Usually Alfred's letters home told his family that he was fine, was doing well and all the other things a young boy writes about from boarding school. His letters expressed concern for his family during the terrible influenza epidemic of 1919. He reassured them that the flu had not hit the seminary. Shortly thereafter, his next letter described the priests and seminarians succumbing to the illness: how sick everyone was, how local women came to nurse the sick and care for the well. All survived.

At seventeen he took his vows as a Franciscan friar, received the simple brown robe of St. Francis of Assisi, his great idol, and a new name. Tony was now Alfred, the name the world would know him by. In 1927 he completed his studies and at twenty-three, was—according to canon law—too young to be ordained. Again he insisted. A dispensation from the Vatican was granted, and on June 11, 1927, he was ordained at the Old Mission. He said his first Mass the following day in his home parish, St. Elizabeth's in Oakland. After more studies in Santa Barbara, he was offered the opportunity to study canon law and theology in Rome. He asked not to go, stating he was too young!

He became the pastor of San Rafael's Church in then-rural Goleta, north of Santa Barbara. It was a poor parish, serving mostly Mexican laboring people and their families. There were great needs and great poverty. Alfred immediately took action, which would be typical of his whole life. He asked his father to come down to help design and build a new church and social hall. He organized recreational opportunities for the children. He started a sports program. He got contributions from Santa Barbara residents to buy equipment for football and baseball. Goleta was a forerunner of what he would do later in life.

The following year, he was again offered study in Rome (which was extremely unusual), and this time he accepted. The Cheney family of Hartford, Connecticut, were great friends of the young priest. They spent the winter season in Santa Barbara. The rest of the year they left their California car for the Franciscan Friars to drive in their absence. When they heard of Alfred's upcoming trip, they paid the passage from New York to Bremen, Germany. They also gave him funds to travel about during summer vacations plus a movie camera and film to record his trips. Alfred was able to visit Germany, France, England, Spain, Portugal and Palestine while in Europe during the turbulent 1930s.

This was Alfred's longest journey yet, from California to Rome. First by train to New York, then by ship to Bremen, where he was met by a cousin who, years later, still remembered the wide-brimmed hat Alfred wore, typical of American priests then. A visit to relatives in Alhausen followed. He was greeted as a returning native son. The pastor asked him to say Mass and preach a sermon. His German was not up to a spiritual message so he simply told of his family, who had migrated some forty years before, what they did and how they lived. It was a great success. Visits to the "Old Country" were much rarer then than now.

Alfred loved telling of being taken around from house to house: "Thirty-four cups of coffee in one day!" He never told how he slept that night.

From Germany he went on to Rome to Antonianum University to specialize in canon law and theology. It was a difficult first year. He became ill and suffered from a deep depression. There was a new language, a very different culture, great poverty and a whole different world than he had known. In one letter to his brother, he wrote how he was planning his return home and thinking of the great joy the reunion with his family would bring. He apologized for not writing more but said he was busy and that he had adopted a rather different attitude: "If I can't write today, I'll do it tomorrow. I find this European spirit to be of great value at times. After all, life is not a rush—life is enjoying each moment. If each moment is occupied with thinking of the next 50 or 60 moments, not even one moment is enjoyed."

He recovered from his illness and depression, did extremely well in his work and received his degree, Lector Generalis, the equivalent of a doctorate, right on schedule. He returned to America via Germany. On his way he met Teresa Neumann in her Bavarian village. She had created a worldwide sensation with her stigmata—that is, wounds that would appear on her hands and feet during Lent, like the wounds of Christ. She is said to have told Alfred that he would walk with the great and famous and would suffer great sorrows. In Italy he had already met Padre Pio, a monk who also carried the stigmata.

One funny story: The university operated on Italian time. Classes began very early in the morning and ended around 11AM. The main meal of the day with wine followed. Then it was siesta time. Father slept, but the heat, the heavy meal, the wine . . . he slept straight through his late afternoon classes, much to his embarrassment.

One cousin recalled that on his return to the United States, Alfred said he wanted to help the poor. It may have been a chance remark but seems to have been a portent of the future. Europe in the 1930s must have been a terrible shock to a man of his sensibilities.

HOME AGAIN

God is love—trust in His goodness.
—Alfred

In Santa Barbara again, any hopes of working with the poor would have to wait. Alfred was assigned to teach canon law, theology and liturgy, the purpose of his studies in Rome. He was a popular teacher, because his classes were never dull or routine. He acted out all the parts and made his examples simple and concrete. He demanded opinions from all his students and made all of them participate in discussions.

At the same time, he served as a canon lawyer to Bishop Buddy of San Diego. Father Floyd observed that "Alfred developed the cold letter of law to a heartwarming charity."

He eventually became Master of Studies of the Seminaries of Santa Barbara, San Miguel and San Luis Rey. He was Dean of Studies of the Franciscan province of Santa Barbara in charge of houses of study on the Pacific Coast.

While he was teaching at the Seminary as early as 1934, he was appalled at the terrible toll the Great Depression was taking on people—especially the poor. It was a situation made to order for Alfred. Quickly he started a sports program for young people—football teams, baseball teams, basketball teams. Interest grew when one young man told another of the program. A regular series of games was developed. Coaches volunteered their time. The city of Santa Barbara bought team uniforms better than those of the local high school. The American Legion band participated by providing marching music for their games.

ST. MARY'S CENTER

I am happy that God is using me as a tool.
—Alfred

Alfred was always interested in getting people together, getting them involved and enjoying themselves, doing things instead of getting into trouble. Word of this got around the Santa Barbara community. Walter Cortez and his son had a dry cleaning business in the Haley Street district, a poor low-rent area where Hispanic and African-American kids were cutting school and getting into trouble. One day Cortez called Alfred. "We should have a place down here for the young kids who have no one to teach them anything."

Cortez owned a piece of property across the street from his business, an old building he was willing to give Alfred. A small organization started to help fix it up and paint it. A club for young people—called St. Mary's Center—was organized. High schoolers, elementary age students, and even little ones, preschoolers, started coming. There were groups for boys and for girls. Two women from the community volunteered to supervise and organize the girls' club. They had a sports program, parties, hikes, beach parties and even a snow outing.

Men volunteered to take charge of the boys' groups. They had a winning football team (the Hornets), a basketball team and Alfred's favorite, a baseball team. They organized a band, had get-togethers and religious instruction. There was a first-aid clinic staffed by local doctors for young people who had no medical treatment of any kind and an employment agency that got jobs for the kids even during the Depression. St. Mary's was making a difference in the Haley Street district. Membership in the two clubs was nearly 1000 young people. The kids were having fun and doing constructive things.

The Santa Barbara community, then as now, was very affluent. The people loved Alfred and helped him with money and time. This was the work which took his heart, soul and all his spare time. The youth center was a very successful going concern, filling a great need.

One evening Father got a call from Archbishop MacIntire's office, asking him to come down to Los Angeles. Once there, he heard: "Father, you have done a wonderful thing there in the Haley Street district, but these clubs, they are in the Guadeloupe Parish, and you are in the Old Mission Parish way up on the hill. I want you to turn St. Mary's Center over to Father Kelly of Guadeloupe now. He will take it from here. We'll continue to do your good work, and we thank you for all that you have done."

The whole thing collapsed in about a year. The girls' building was sold; the boys' center is still there, now owned by Catholic Charities. Food is served to the poor once a day and there is still an employment agency. A thrift shop heavily supported by the community is the main money-raising activity. It is closely watched by the locals for the very fine things donated from all the parishes of Santa Barbara.

Alfred never uttered a word of complaint, but he never went to Haley Street again. Friends and family knew what a great loss it was to him and what pain it caused him. He was still teaching but needed something else to fill his time and heart, so he gardened. He took out his disappointment by putting his hands into the soil. Many remember how he raised marvelous vegetables.

Along with his work at the Seminary, he was always deeply involved in the Santa Barbara community. Many local people came to him for spiritual, moral and financial advice. One such was Nellie Covarrubbias, whom Father knew from his days as pastor at Goleta. The small town of Gaviota where she lived was part of his first parish. Mrs. Covarrubbias was a member of a Spanish land grant family of early California history. Such land grants by the Spanish viceroy of New Spain deeded land to men who had served in the army or had done some other service for the government. The patents are marvelous to read since they deeded land "so-and-so many leagues from the mountains to the sea." Sometimes "as far as the eye can see." Nellie in Gaviota had inherited the family home and adjoining property from El Capitan to Refugio beaches on the Coast. Now in her sixties and a widow, she came to Father Alfred.

"Shell Oil wants to drill for oil on my land, and I'm afraid of what will happen to my property up there. I'm a widow, and I don't know what to do, Father."

"Oh, don't be afraid. It won't be a problem. We'll find someone to keep an eye on it. And I'll keep my eyes on it too. Don't worry."

Father knew someone who could be trusted and who would watch out for Nellie's interests. "I don't want anyone to get that poor lady's money."

Shell Oil Company drilled. The first gusher came in. Alfred was called, drove out to the site, blessed the well and called it St. Anthony. More and more wells came in. Each got blessed and was named for a saint until there were twenty-nine wells, all with saints' names. Nellie's royalties were nearly $1 million per year! This in 1930s dollars.

One day, an attorney came to the Old Mission to speak to Alfred. He had some papers. "Father, I want you to sign these papers."

"What are they?"

"Mrs. Covarrubbias is making you half owner of her oil wells."

"I can't sign that. I'm a Franciscan and have taken a vow of poverty. If I sign that, I would have to leave the Order."

"Do you know what you are doing? You are to own half those oil wells. Half a million dollars per year!"

"Let me get my superior."

He did, and the man confirmed what Alfred had said, adding, "It would violate his vow of poverty."

The attorney found it all very difficult to understand.

The pumping continued for 6–8 years. Then in February 1942—during World War II—a Japanese submarine shelled the Santa Barbara Coast, attempting to hit the oil tanks on this property. The Japanese guns missed their target and hit an unused water tank farther up the hill. It was the first time enemy shells had hit the continental United States since 1814, when the British shelled the East Coast. As a result of the shelling, the government ordered the oil pumping on that site shut down for the duration. After the war, pumping started up again on a limited basis. But by then the companies preferred to drill offshore where they could tap into some of the same underground reserves from a distance.

On Mrs. Covarrubbias's death, one-third of her property was willed to her brother and sister, one-third to her second husband and one-third to the Franciscan Order. Today there is a limited amount of pumping still continuing on "Father's Oil Wells."

Alfred's brother Frank Boeddeker's comment on the oil well story was: "He loved to see people come out on something like that, especially people who had had little or nothing. He loved working with people. He never wanted anything for himself. I learned a lot from him. My brother was a wonderful man."

Alfred's work in the seminary and the St. Mary's Center, his duties as canon lawyer and his community efforts took their toll. By 1946 he was tired. He had worked fourteen years to the point of exhaustion. There followed a year's sabbatical, and he did a little parish work and a lot of gardening. Apparently he had a real talent for growing things; his garden flourished. It provided vegetables for the friars, and the leftovers were given away. There were rumors that he had been removed from his posts because he was too strict as a professor, that he was too puritanical, but these comments proved to be without validity. What was very apparent was that he had worked himself to a point where he could not go on.

He never complained. No one in the family heard any murmur. There was never a question of "how did this happen?" Yet Alfred's whole career was gone, his beloved St. Mary's Center and his teaching. He had no idea where he was going, so he gardened, and—typical of Alfred—he put his faith and trust in God.

A NEW OPPORTUNITY

Think big and you will be big. Think small and you will be small.
                    —Alfred

A great career challenge presented itself. The Franciscans decided with World War II over, they would establish a Catholic university in Hankow, China. Alfred asked for the assignment of founding it and being its president. To prepare for this, he returned to the Bay Area and enrolled in the Chinese Language Studies Program at the University of California, Berkeley, studying Mandarin Chinese, Japanese and Russian plus Chinese culture. In spite of his previous studies, he found the Asian languages a challenge.

"I would practice and practice and practice the sounds," he recalled. "So many were almost the same but had totally different meanings depending on the accent. Finally, almost by accident, I would get the right sound. 'Great. Do it again.' then 'Wrong.'"

Consider that Alfred was already fluent in German, Spanish, Italian and French as well as Latin and English.

When one family member asked if such an assignment to China could be dangerous, he replied that a martyr's death would be the best death he could wish for. His aged mother, who had him close by for the first time in many years, was not so sure. One wonderful thing about this assignment was that he was near to her for the year or two she had to live, a great joy to both.

Then came the political whirlwind in China, which closed its doors to all Westerners. Alfred, age 47, was out of a job again. He had no idea what this turning point would bring, but he put his trust in his God and accepted all as God's will. A short time later, he was appointed as pastor to St. Boniface Church. Back to his beginnings—the church where his parents were married and where he was baptized. And this was to be the start of his greatest accomplishments.

Someone pointed out, "At first glance, it seemed to be a waste of talent and training to allocate such an erudite man to such a humble parish." Especially in the Tenderloin. Were they wrong!

JONES STREET

One of the most influential advocates for the poor and the aged throughout the country.
—A reporter, after an
interview with Alfred.

St. Boniface Church had a long tradition of charity in keeping with Franciscan ideals. After the 1906 earthquake and fire, a bread line was organized for survivors of that disaster. During the Great Depression of the 1930s, the Church fed some 700 hungry people a day. Each day at around 7AM, people would file into St. Boniface Auditorium where they got hot coffee, rolls and cereal. In the booming 1940s, with a wartime economy, the operation was halted for a time. But later in the decade, the economic readjustment from wartime to peacetime production resulted in a recession. At the parish door, the Franciscans gave out sandwiches and vouchers, fifty per day in the value of 35 cents. Recipients could buy food at certain restaurants. At the end of the month the Friars would redeem the vouchers. When Alfred discovered that the food was handed out the back doors of these restaurants, he was offended. A better way had to be found. The voucher system was inefficient and the manner in which the food was given out went against his sense of human dignity.

"I thought we just had to do more than give out mere slips of paper," Alfred commented years later.

He pondered the problem. While leading the usual Tuesday night devotions to St. Anthony, Alfred looked up at the statue of his patron and noted that the saint was giving a loaf of bread to a poor man. "Why don't you do that?" was the thought that came to Alfred's mind.

"I told myself it was just a passing fancy, and then it hit me again. 'Why don't you do that?' In my heart, I said to St. Anthony, 'What shall I do?'

"'You do it, and I'll help,' was the message that I got." Later Father modestly referred to this incident as less a miracle than "some kind of inspiration."

Not long afterward, a former auto shop around the corner from the church on Jones Street became available. Immediately after World War II, it had been a surplus military store, but by 1950 that supply of goods had dried up, and the shop was unoccupied. It was almost subterranean space and a mess. There was grease on the floors and walls; electrical wires hung from the ceiling; it was dark and dank. Yet it was the ideal site, right around the corner from St. Boniface on Golden Gate Avenue. It was also a good size: 175 feet long and 50 feet wide. It could seat 280 people at a time, with enough space to cook and serve. No one expected more than 280 men. Father visualized people coming down the stairs (since converted to a ramp). He saw clean Formica-top tables, clean walls, asphalt tile floors, kitchen equipment and food for the hungry. And he saw the hungry eating good, wholesome, hot meals. Best of all, the property already belonged to the Franciscans!

With the help of volunteers, mostly from the many union halls headquartered nearby, the garage was renovated. Carpenters, plumbers, electricians, painters and other skilled workmen gave their time, skill and caring.

First there was the cleaning, then repairs to floors, walls, ceiling, then the plumbing. John Korbus—the head maintenance man of St. Boniface and one of Alfred's lifelong friends—laid the floor tile one by one, very carefully ... a good job so that it would last. It would need to last a long time, for the Dining Room would not be a temporary measure.

The renovation took months. A civic group was organized to underwrite and support the project. Father's backers and supporters were, and would remain, a remarkable group ... leaders of a City which prides itself on civic responsibility. Support came from all sectors: Catholics, Protestants, Masons, people not affiliated with any religious group. Some of his most devoted supporters to the very end of his life were from the prominent Jewish families of the area. Creed had nothing to do with response to the needs of the less fortunate. This was and would remain an ecumenical effort long before that concept became popular. People of means gave money; the poor and the working people gave money, time and labor. All gave love.

Kitchen suppliers donated equipment. Alfred appealed for castoff kitchen and dining utensils—knives, forks, spoons, dishes, cups, glasses—imagine the list. Furniture, tables and chairs. Pots and pans.

Commitments were made that when the time came, there would be food. Bakeries and produce people would donate day-old bread, fruit, vegetables. Dairies, milk. Wholesale butchers, meat. When a North Beach fish dealer was not interested in contributing and word somehow got back to his partner—his sister—she called Alfred and promised, "You get your fish. Ask me."

Alfred explained again and again that these were good men, these men on the streets or living in cheap hotels. They were not just winos who were down and out, but men who had taken a wrong turn somewhere along the line. They needed help to get their lives back on track. But first they needed food. "They've run out of unemployment insurance and public welfare is swamped. Times are tough."

Alfred decided right from the start that this facility would not be called a "soup kitchen"—a term with such a negative connotation and not in keeping with the dignity of people. It raised a picture of long lines of hungry men standing on the street with a bowl in hand, waiting for a ladleful of watery soup, a piece of bread and a cup of coffee. It could not be called a restaurant; that might give the wrong impression.

It would be a Dining Room . . . St. Anthony's Dining Room. It would not have metal trays; that was too institutional. It would have plates—even if breakage had to be considered. It would feel warm, friendly and homelike. It would serve good, hot food with generous portions. It would call its patrons guests, and it would welcome all who were hungry. "We're not just giving charity," Alfred announced, "We are going to give good men hot meals and all the help we can to get them going again. St. Francis loved the poor, you know, and so does the good Lord."

On October 4, 1950, the feast of St. Francis—the patron saint of the City of San Francisco—the Dining Room was formally opened with a blessing by Bishop Merlin Gilfoyle, in his first official act as bishop.

Now, what if you gave a party and everyone came and brought two extra people? That was opening day. It was estimated that maybe a hundred men would be served each day at first. Based on the statistics of the former bread line, that would reach 350 in a few months.

How wrong they were! The first day around 380 came. By the end of the month, St. Anthony's was feeding at least 300–400 people each day. Within six months there were 1200–1500 people per day in the line. The hidden need had been there all along, but it was not visible until an adequate response was made available. That response was now in place, available to all and open five days per week at 45 Jones Street.

Several soup kitchens had operated in the area before, sponsored by storefront missions. They had offered the hungry a bowl of hot soup, two slices of bread and a cup of coffee in exchange for prayer, singing and a sermon or two. No singing, no food. Alfred was appalled by such actions. He felt it was neither Christian nor charitable. He lived his faith in his work. He did not try to coerce others into believing as he believed; he would not make hungry men go through the motions of singing hymns or saying prayers they did not believe. He would not insult them by preaching at them. He blessed the food; that was it. The patrons of St. Anthony were guests and would be treated as one treats guests in one's home. His guests and friends would eat good, nutritious food in a warm, clean place. There would be no questions, no judgments, no sermons. The whole operation of serving, eating, entering and leaving always moved smoothly, without supervision and with no hassles.

A typical story from those early days was of a young man from Chicago—arrested for drunkenness and just out of jail—who went to St. Anthony's and got a meal. Afterward he said, "Okay, when do we get down on our knees?"

"You don't here," a worker replied.

"When's the lecture?"

"There isn't any."

"What's the gimmick?"

The volunteer pointed to the Latin inscription on the wall: *"Caritate Dei."*

"What does it mean?"

"Out of love for God."

THE MIRACLE OF
JONES STREET

Hunger relieved. Hope restored.
> —A sign in St. Anthony Dining Room

At first, little notice was taken of this unique dining room. Newspapers reported there was this St. Anthony Dining Room in the Tenderloin which gave free meals. The articles tended to be very small. The powers of the City who were watching and waiting did not believe that such a venture could make it. Feeding all those people without any help from federal, state, city or Church funds? Just private donations? The line was getting longer every day. "No, just give it time," the "wise" ones said. "The project is just too big." Even in the archbishop's office it was whispered: "Give it three months."

But the Dining Room kept on feeding people every day—fewer at the beginning of the month, then more at the end when people had used up their limited funds.

Thanksgiving and Christmas were just around the corner. Father Alfred decided that these feasts would be celebrated as they should be celebrated: turkey, dressing, peas, mashed potatoes, salad, nuts, candy and ice cream and—of course—a cup of coffee. No one could have any idea how many would come. Careful preparations had to be made. Thanksgiving was a great success. Next, Christmas . . . more than 2000 people came!

They were entertained by the Boys' Choir of St. Boniface School. Father greeted each and every one. It was a real Christmas dinner with turkey and trimmings, a stunning success and the beginning of a long tradition.

For the six-month anniversary, other guests came: the sheriff, the police chief, the fire chief, the postmaster, the auxiliary bishop. Important people were beginning to take note of this remarkable establishment. More and more, Father was involving the political, social and humanitarian leaders as well as the ordinary citizens of San Francisco in a worthwhile effort to help their less-blessed brothers and sisters. His Board of Directors began to sound like the power heart of the City: the mayor, the archbishop, judges, lawyers, doctors, prominent business leaders. Alfred would call on these people regularly and ask for advice, for help, for support. He was involving everyone, people from all walks of life and from every religious, ethnic and political persuasion. He was not afraid to ask for advice. What he never directly asked for was financial support.

Public interest, too, was slowly being aroused. The press as early as 1951 dubbed St. Anthony Dining Room the "Miracle of Jones Street." It had not closed its doors or turned away anyone for lack of food in the year it had been open. It never has. It seems no matter how many come, there is always enough food. It has always been a regular "loaves and fishes" project.

Father organized a club to help finance the costs of the food and overhead. He asked people to give a dollar or more per month. Many people could give that. Just one buck. That dollar could make a difference. One did not have to be wealthy to help. Anyone could help.

Cans asking for donations were placed in many public places, including bars. The local labor unions were instrumental in getting this drive organized. It was all-important. In six months the Dining Room was serving an average of 1200 meals per day. Not bad for a dining room without a cash register and no public or Church funds to support it—only donations from people who cared and who wanted to do something to help those less fortunate.

In addition to getting the Dining Room started that first year, Alfred as pastor completed the Serra Center, which included a lending library of 7000 volumes, a credit union, a family guild to help young parents financially, a free employment agency, a social center for men and women under thirty and another for people over thirty. The Center also had offices for the administration of the Dining Room and Franciscan Marian Commission, which was part of a national and international organization to encourage devotion to the Blessed Virgin Mary. This devotion was always very close to Alfred's heart.

Alfred spent a good deal of time and effort on his first annual report to the Board of Directors. He took the members of the board to lunch as a token of his gratitude for all they did for him. And he publicly praised their work. This would be a pattern for the many years he was the director of the St. Anthony Dining Room, always letting people know they had done a good job and that he was grateful.

In the 1950s, someone wrote that "the St. Anthony Dining Room was an agency which was begun on faith alone and which sprang almost overnight into one of San Francisco's largest charitable enterprises."

THINGS START TO HAPPEN

The line forms early for the 11AM opening. It is quiet, orderly, humorous. Some stand straight, some avert their eyes, others look down and then away.
—An observer

Very shortly things started changing at the Dining Room. Women and children were now coming. They had slowly begun to realize that St. Anthony's was a place of dignity and respect where they could be comfortable and not be threatened.

Jobs were found for 200 men in the first months of the Dining Room's operation. Father Alfred and his staff had many contacts, making it possible to get work for men from "the line." The next logical step was the establishment of the St. Anthony Employment Agency, which over the years would find jobs, temporary and permanent, for thousands of people. Jobs would get these people back into life; back into the mainstream.

With the huge number of guests coming to the Dining Room every day, it was quickly apparent that the Franciscan Friars could not do all the serving. Additional servers and helpers were needed. Such a group required organization. In time there were 415 volunteer women in the St. Anthony Helpers. They served the food, taking trays to the elderly and the infirm who could not

33

stand in line. They picked up the plates afterward and cleaned the Dining Room. These women came from all walks of life: some were wives of prominent men, some women of independent means, others working women, some retired or widowed with time to help others. These servers were the backbone of the Dining Room. For them there was no glamour, no photos in the newspapers, no stories. But Father Alfred recognized what they did. Once a year they were his guests at a luncheon where they were presented awards and recognized for their great help and service.

Among Father's early and most devoted supporters were Fred and Barbara Meiswinkel, German immigrants who started a construction company and were very successful. They felt they owed San Francisco for their success, and their way of repaying this was to help the poor of the City.

Barbara was an important part of the Dining Room Auxiliary from its earliest days. She was one of the most faithful servers in the St. Anthony Helpers. When plans were made for Father's ninetieth birthday celebration, he said, "Oh, a cake is all that I need." But Barbara—almost ninety herself—said, "No, Father, it will be done right." She personally made most of the refreshments for a rather large party of friends and family. She passed away only a few months after Alfred, her good friend of so many years.

People from the line often volunteered to be among the 20 dishwashers, floor-moppers and food-stirrers needed. Along with the St. Anthony Helpers, these people kept the place spotlessly clean. The Dining Room was a going concern. It was people helping people to help themselves.

Father put it very simply in an interview:. "I am practical. I know sentiment and sympathy are not enough. I know that an efficient organization accomplishes more than any individual. Therefore, I try to get a clear picture of a situation. I visualize what can be done under the circumstances. Then I organize groups to accomplish the purpose."

MORE SUPPORT

It has been said of Alfred that he worked for the poor, but he never offended or envied the rich. A rare person.
—Gene Benedetti

The problems were enormous; the needs were enormous. The manager in those days gathered used clothes and stored them in a closet in the back of the kitchen. If someone was pretty ragged, he would give that person clean clothes. When the staff had time, they would cut the hair of the guests. "Make them feel they still have dignity."

But always there was just so much that could be done. Funds and resources were limited. Father would do more, much more—more than he ever dreamed possible—but it would take time.

A thrift shop was started, at first selling clothes and other items, with the money going to help support the Dining Room. When the problem of clothing the poor became greater, the shop simply gave the clothes away. Today there is a regular routine where in the mornings men can get a clean set of clothing. In the afternoon, families are welcome, and in the evening, women can get a change of clean new clothes. Furniture is also given to people to help furnish their homes.

On the first anniversary of the Dining Room, the cook pointed out to the press several men working in the kitchen. "Those two both have chief engineer's papers in the Merchant Marine. That one is an artist. The old man over there was once a personal guard for the King of Italy. They work here until they can get on their feet again."

When asked, Alfred commented that the Franciscans had never insisted upon respect, yet in the first year no one had ever been disrespectful to him, the Franciscans or the St. Anthony Helpers.

By the end of 1952, the millionth meal was served with a good deal of media attention and with many city leaders in attendance. They dished up mashed potatoes and whatever else was on the menu. This too would become a tradition. The press was taking more note. The millionth person received gifts, had his picture taken with Alfred and city officials and had his fifteen minutes of fame.

Herb Caen, a member of the press, would be one of Alfred's strongest supporters through the long years. Some might call him a columnist, but most would call him a legend and "Mr. San Francisco." Regularly, he mentioned the coming events at St. Anthony's and the needs—especially for holiday turkeys. He would put in a plug for something, tell a humorous story that happened at Jones Street, or simply remind the readers of the *San Francisco Chronicle* that this remarkable enterprise was ongoing.

A typical story of the support Alfred had is told by Frank Schepergerdes, who worked for Father for thirty-five years and developed a deep personal relationship with the priest. "I took the truck to Union City for repairs. This was in the late 1950s. I drove in the shop. There was no name on the door of the truck. The shop foreman asked, 'Where are you from?' I told him. When he was sure exactly who I was and who the truck belonged to, he whistled to the men in the shop. 'Hey, I want you guys to a have a look at this truck. This is where you are giving your money to. This is part of it; these wheels belong to St. Anthony's.' I had no idea what he was talking about. 'Get this guy fixed up. You know what to do.' They fixed the truck in about an hour. I asked how much. 'Forget about it. All these guys in the shop give to St. Anthony's. Hat goes around once a month and everyone puts something in.'"

It was not just food, clothing and money that were needed. The kitchen needed more and more equipment. Dohrman's Kitchen Supply, a wholesaler, would call. "We are selling some new equipment and the used stuff is being traded in. Do you want it? We are getting steam kettles, big tanks, flat pans for the oven, bowls for salad." Of course.

Refrigeration equipment, freezers, cold storage units, plumbing supplies, cleaning compounds, ventilation equipment and paint . . . the list went on and on. Everything was needed. Brady's Electrical Supply was an enormous help. Ed Brady, a prominent Mason, was a good friend and supporter. Scatena-York Refrigeration Company was called in for advice and to redesign the refrigeration equipment. Jim Scatena became a lifelong friend and supporter of Alfred.

What was the Dining Room like? Clean, clean, clean. It's the same today. Fifteen hundred people or more—some clean, others not—go through that line, and yet, the Dining Room is spotless. Tables and chairs are kept in good repair. The walls, painted by a Marin County muralist, are covered with country scenes. Since it's in a basement, windows are painted in, with curtains blowing in the fresh air. "Outside" there are trees, grass, flowers and sunshine.

Throughout the room there are real ferns and potted plants; soft music plays in the background.

Frank Schepergerdes recalls: "He often would say, 'We don't have new things. We don't have the things that some people would love to have in a kitchen and a dining room. But there is no excuse for not having it clean, no excuse whatever.' He personally would see to it that it would remain that way. He would often come to the Dining Room before serving to see that everything was as he wanted it. After the noon meal had been served and before everyone went home, he would walk through to be sure that no one missed anything. He always had that personal interest. 'You can't run anything from an office. You have to be amongst them.' He was right from the start."

As early as 1954, the Dining Room was presented a Gold Certificate of Merit on its cleanliness by the director of Public Health of San Francisco. It was the Department's highest award and one treasured by Alfred.

In 1958 new, shining, bright stainless steel kitchen equipment was blessed by Alfred, a gift from Mrs. George Cameron in memory of her husband, the publisher of the *San Francisco Chronicle*. She also provided the meal for the 1700 diners that day. Since it was St. Patrick's Day, the menu featured corned beef and cabbage.

And Father always had his sense of humor. When he was describing the Dining Room operation to relatives in Germany shortly after it opened, one good housewife wanted to know who washes "all those dishes." Alfred answered with a smile, "I do." She was not convinced but her children caught the twinkle in his eye and thought it a great joke.

THE GUESTS

Who are the people who eat here? The hungry—old and young—the shabby, the presentable, the clean, the otherwise.

—Alfred

A radio ad in the 1970s with Father's voice summed up the whole concept of St. Anthony Dining Room (popularly known as "Tony's Place"): "There is an exclusive dining room you may not have heard about. To qualify you might try being old, sick or broken in spirit. It's called St. Anthony Dining Room and it's free. The place is supported by ordinary people, not the church or anything . . . so if you're hungry drop over. If not, send a couple of bucks. Then someone else can eat." Many said this was the most dramatic ad the Dining Room ever had.

So who were the men, women and children who lined up early and patiently waited in line an hour or two to eat there? When the question was put to Alfred, he snapped back with a show of temper not often seen in this gentle priest.

"What right do we have to ask that? With most, something is broken—hidden. We try to help them, restore their dignity. Prodding into their lives would be rude, sacrilegious. And we frown on sermons here."

They were hungry. That was the common denominator.

In the early 1950s, Alfred commented, "They are men from all walks of life and all professions. They're down on their luck, and our job is to treat them so they are aware of their dignity as men."

In the early days of the Dining Room's operation, a regular patron was a 67-year-old veteran of World War I who had lost an eye and part of his leg when he was pinned down by machine gun fire at the Battle of St. Mihiel. From subsequent wars, men disabled physically or with their souls destroyed by those experiences have been regular guests. There was a graduate engineer from Northwestern University who lived in his truck and ate at the Dining Room regularly. No one knew what brought him there. No one at the Dining Room would ever ask. In the 1950s, it was the winos of Skid Row and more recently, the drug-users who would come for food and a moment to be a person again. Today, it is families with small children who need the help of a few good free meals to make it on their limited incomes.

Anna Bosset at eighty-six was still a handsome woman with what people call "good bones." She had been a Hollywood bit player and appeared in movies with William S. Hart, of whom she said, "He was a fine gentleman." Hart was probably the first Hollywood cowboy hero, long before Tom Mix and long, long before John Wayne.

In 1974, Anna Bosset was the eleventh million diner at the Miracle of Jones Street. When Father Alfred stopped her in the line and told her of the honor, she said, "God bless you all."

"God bless *you*, madam," replied Mayor Joseph Alioto as he ladled out a heaping serving of turkey a la king. Archbishop Joseph McGucken served her vegetables and salad.

Over ice cream and coffee, she told the press how her $100 a month pension left her no money for food, so she was a regular patron of Tony's Place—absolutely dependent on the warm, well-balanced meals served at the Dining Room. "As if things aren't bad enough, I've been mugged and had my purse snatched several times. But I can still put up a fight."

Another millionth recipient, an Italian immigrant, was a fine cabinetmaker, but there had not been much call for his craft in recent years. He happily ate his meal of turkey, potatoes, salad and ice cream, took his gifts of a suit, razor and cigarettes and planned to continue eating at the Dining Room Without a Cash Register until he could find suitable work.

In the early 1950s the San Francisco police chief lived in neighboring San Mateo and kept telling his neighbor, a woman of considerable means, about the Dining Room. "No," she said, "there is no such thing. You get something for nothing. You don't have to say anything. You don't have to pray. No, there is no such place." But she would return to the story. "Where is this place? You go in, pick up a tray, get your food, eat and leave? I don't believe it."

Finally one day she dressed in very ordinary clothes, went to San Francisco, got in line, took her tray through, was greeted with smiles, sat down and ate. No one said anything. She then went to the front office and wrote a check for $5,000 to the Dining Room. Quite a tip!

While shopping at Rochester Big and Tall, a men's clothing store, a cousin of Father's was talking to the store owner about the Dining Room. A prominent basketball player overheard their conversation and told them many of the girls he knew that worked the streets gave to St. Anthony's when they were making money.

When they hit a "slump in business," they would eat at "Tony's Place" and feel that they had already paid for their meals.

In the late 1960s, when San Francisco became a mecca for many of the nation's discontented youth—who quickly got the names "hippies" and "flower children"—there was a backlash against them. A newspaper columnist asked one such young person how he could live without any money. The answer was simple: "Eat at St. Anthony Dining Room." Thereupon, many patrons turned to Alfred and told him he would receive no more contributions from them ... "Let those hippies work!"

Alfred wrote letters to the editors of the major San Francisco newspapers, telling the public it was no secret that their free meals went to the needy of any race, color or ethnic origin. The guests were saints and sinners. The Dining Room was following the example of the loaves and fishes. "And nowhere was it recorded that Jesus commanded His disciples to refrain from giving away food to Pharisees, Samaritans, thieves, gentiles, publicans or the unclean. He simply fed the hungry. We try to do likewise."

Frank Boeddeker, Father's younger brother, noted, "Young kids would come through the line. I would think, I'm glad it isn't one of mine. They looked as if no one ever loved them. I just wanted to say to them, 'Come here, kid. I want to give you a good hug.'"

One woman told a poignant story. Her husband had lost his job, and they could no longer afford the place where they were living; so they—husband, wife and three children—moved into a studio in the Tenderloin. It was terribly small but they could pay the rent. But they could not always afford to buy food, so they ate at St. Anthony's four or five times a week. "It's in the Dining Room that my youngest has found enough room to walk. I never thought my 14-month-old would be taking her first steps any place other than home, but she's been learning to walk here. As her mom, it's hard not to have this happening in our own home. Our family is making the best of the situation. I can only hope that her baby steps lead to a brighter future for her and all of us."

Businessmen in the area often come in for a cup of coffee and offer $5.

Each year Charlie Chananudeck—owner of Annie's Seafood Restaurant on Mission Street—donates a day's gross receipts to St. Anthony's, as he has done for several years out of gratitude. When he arrived from Thailand, he had no job, no home and no money. "St. Anthony's saved my life." A day's gross one year was $1200.

In the mid 1970s, with inflation rampant, a "Skidrowgue" (a term coined by columnist Herb Caen) called out to Alfred: "Hey, Father, I wanna congratulate you on holding the line. You've got the only cafeteria in town that hasn't raised its prices."

Another mother said, "Everyone is so kind and the food is so good. My little girl loves it here. She says we're going visiting on days we come here. But my husband has a job in Los Angeles now and has sent us bus tickets to join him. You've been good to us."

As a sign of the times today, a third of the Dining Room is set aside for families. And the rest is for the handicapped, alcoholics, derelicts, drifters, transvestites, prostitutes and hundreds of other people down on their luck who survive by eating here. And there's always space for the elderly whose pensions just don't make it to the end of the month.

On Thanksgiving 1984, a well-to-do contractor from Livermore (across the Bay) got his reluctant wife and children into the car and drove to San Francisco. There they stood at the end of the line of people waiting to eat at the Dining Room. When people saw the children, they told them to move up to the front of the line. The family was amazed that people so down and out still had concern for others. "I wanted my family to see the way a lot of people have to live," the contractor explained. "I wanted them to understand that because of a lack of a job or a health problem, people are at the mercy of charity. I intend to make a donation. I did not think there would be this many people."

On one occasion San Francisco socialite Pat Montandon and her then husband Al Wilsey, along with Father Miles Riley, were at St. Anthony's for lunch. They were there to discuss and call attention to a documentary film on world hunger called *Excuse Me, America*, which was to be shown at Grace Episcopal Cathedral. Pat was elegant in a white wool skirt and a pearl silk blouse. One puzzled regular called out, "Did you get your purse ripped off, lady? Is that why you're here?"

CHRISTMAS

In order to keep love, you have to give it away.
—Alfred

Christmas at St. Anthony's is always special. On that day some people come who *could* pay for a dinner but wish for the feeling of warmth and kindness and family that is the Dining Room. Once for Christmas someone sent corsages for all the women eating there that day, and some of them wept; it had been years since anyone sent them flowers. Another time a person sent Christmas cards for all the elderly guests . . . with $5 enclosed in each.

One Christmas 4000 meals had been served. It was the end of a long day. A few hundred guests and helpers remained to clean up. A man walked over to the piano and began to play—wonderfully. Everyone began to sing, clap, move and dance. It was old favorite tunes and traditional carols. A matronly black woman in a simple blue smock with a red bandana on her head started to dance. Then an elderly white man beat out rhythm with two spoons, put them down and danced with the lady. Everyone knew this was getting special. "We all let our hair down. We were all one family: brothers and sisters, young and old, black, white, brown, yellow, red . . . handsome or once so . . . guests, helpers. Children with eyes of wonder were kissing wrinkled elderly cheeks. Every face was smiling, every eye wet. It was a rare moment of love, joy and sharing. A black man came over to a white man and said, "Brother, this is the best Christmas ever. I really feel wanted and part of the family." Another ventured, "We were really brothers and sisters . . . the family of God."

THE SERVERS

San Francisco has immense social problems: homelessness, AIDS, the poverty of many people who live side by side with all this abundance. There is a lot of suffering here.
            —Archbishop John Quinn

Who serves these people? At least two archbishops, assorted bishops, a vice president of the United States, U.S. Senators, several members of Congress, every mayor of the city, police chiefs, fire chiefs and just plain folks have all helped dish up the food.

Film stars too: June Lockhart, a good friend of Father's, served many times. Jane Wyman of *Falcon Crest* fame (she was serving long before that television series); James Garner, star of the television series *Maverick* and *The Rockford Files*; and James Arness of *Gunsmoke* have all served the guests. San Francisco Giants baseball great Willie McCovey has filled the plates of the hungry coming through the line.

Senator Dianne Feinstein, as mayor of San Francisco, did a great deal. She served regularly and came to many functions. Other mayors, too, have lent a hand, starting with George Christopher, then John Shelley, Joe Alioto, George Moscone, Art Agnos and Frank Jordan. State Senator Milton Marks and his family often come on holidays to serve, unannounced.

48

"Sugar Mary" worked six days a week for more than twelve years, spooning sugar into the cups of God's souls, as someone called them. She greeted everyone with a smile and a quip. "I love it here. I could have got a job elsewhere, but I wouldn't have liked it as well. No one knows this but I think I own the place. Sometimes a real young fella will come by, and he'll be sort of forlorn, and I'll try to make him laugh. I'll say to him, 'I thought you'd never get here.'"

Josephine Gagan, the kind of native San Franciscan who wouldn't dream of going downtown without a hat and gloves, shared a wonderful story. She and a friend were walking through Union Square in the center of the City, when a street person called out, "Hiya Josephine." Sniffed the friend, "How does that, er, bum know your first name?"

"Oh, that's Charlie. We have lunch together every Wednesday." At St. Anthony's, she meant, where she was the oldest volunteer. When she died at ninety-four—less than a week after putting in her usual stint—she asked her son to be sure to get a good volunteer to take her place at the Dining Room.

Students from a San Francisco prep school spent their vacations working in the Dining Room. After viewing the poverty and need, one commented to local columnist Stephanie Salter: "We can't let things like this happen in our society. This is terrible. People need help. Maybe a few do cheat but the greater number are in need, so let a few slip through and don't make such a big deal about it."

Alfred's Good Helper Code for the volunteers was: "The good helper expresses goodwill to guests. Our guests, no matter what their temporary condition may be, are still our brothers and sisters in the great human family. The greater their distress, the more they need a friendly word, a cheerful smile, some sign to show that they are warmly welcomed."

Grace has always been said before the food is served. Usually Alfred or one of the Franciscan Fathers said the prayer, but one day no priest was available, so a Secular Franciscan was asked to step in. Perhaps a bit flustered, he started out well enough . . . "Bless us, O Lord, and these Thy gifts and . . . to the Republic for which it stands, one nation under God, indivisible, with liberty and justice for all. Amen. " And with that, everyone sat down to eat.

For many years the juvenile court ordered offenders to serve "charity time" at the Dining Room. Later this was cancelled by the courts.

On its forty-fifth anniversary (in 1995), the St. Anthony Foundation announced that more than seven million hours of labor and love had been volunteered.

A longtime friend of Father's recalled, "Alfred was a familiar sight in the Tenderloin, always in his brown robe—which others had long ago given up for T-shirts and jeans; he wore his with great joy. With his gentle manner, he would stop to talk to pimps, drug dealers, prostitutes and the simple down-and-out. Even when confined to a wheelchair, he could be seen on Golden Gate Avenue or around the corner on Jones Street . . . laughing, smiling, talking and encouraging his guests."

TURKEY, ANYONE?

We must maintain the right atmosphere here, including personal attitudes that show our guests that we welcome them, that we respect their dignity as human beings worthy of our love and goodwill . . . that life is worth living.
                                    —Alfred

Once a year shortly before Thanksgiving, a big drive was made for turkeys. Enough birds were collected to provide for Thanksgiving and have enough left over for Christmas. The public responded with money or, in many cases, actual dressed turkeys delivered to the Dining Room. People in affluent nearby areas—such as Marin County across the Golden Gate Bridge, San Mateo County to the south or Oakland and suburbs across the Bay—made drives to collect turkeys and take them to the Dining Room. Sometimes they brought in the "fixings" that make these holidays special.

What else came in on an unsolicited basis? Wild geese and rabbits from hunters were often donated, which "friends in the butcher business take care of for us," meaning they cleaned and dressed the game and prepared it for cooking.

Paul—a fine young man but a bit wild at that time— was working as a driver for a large deli. One day when he and two friends reported for work, the boss of the kitchen threw three cooked roast beefs to them. "Here. You guys are hungry. Take these." Wow! Off they went, figuring the chef must be mad at the owner. They discussed their situation: "Hey, these are stolen goods." / "Yeah, what do we do?" They took the roasts to St. Anthony's and handed them to the staff. "Here." / "Thanks." / "Okay, we're clear."

Wild pigs were spreading all over Marin County, getting into the water supply, rooting up wild orchids on Mt. Tamalpais and generally destroying the environment. Finally, in June 1985, three were killed, and the wild porkers found their way to the tables of . . . naturally, St. Anthony's.

Another very unusual gift was a Godiva Chocolates donation at $13.50 per pound . . . $250 worth.

Blum's, a super-fancy bakery and restaurant (no longer in business), would send boxes and boxes of cakes, cream cakes, ten-layer cakes, cream puffs, custard-filled cakes . . . all day-old—and for Blum's, of course, not saleable—but still delicious.

One day someone from the American President Lines (then running passenger liners to Hawaii and cruise ships to many ports of the Pacific) called. "Send a truck down to pier so-and-so." Alfred was mystified, but he sent the truck and all was soon cleared up. The passenger line had a delay in its departure time, so the bon voyage party was cancelled. All the party food, canapés, and hors d'oeuvres were sent to the Dining Room, whose guests ate canapés three at a time with great pleasure.

Typically, a call might come from someone in the wholesale produce market. Lettuce would be flooding the market, so the owner would say simply "Get it outta here." So 50–100 crates of lettuce would be sent to the Dining Room. Or fruit that had been in the cold storage when a new shipment was coming in . . . "Get it outta here" and off would go crates of fruit to Jones Street.

Ships from Alaska Packers Company would come into the port of San Francisco. "Father, we'll send you some fish." Fish would arrive in piles. The Dining Room staff would clean and freeze them, and the Dining Room would be supplied with fish for months.

In the very early days, Kilpatrick's Bread Company announced they would send day-old bread and asked, "Father, how many people do you expect per day?"

"I have no idea." The bakery thereupon sent fifty loaves of bread and the next day another fifty. In those days the Dining Room did not have great freezer capacity. "What are we going to do with all this bread? We can't waste it." So Alfred sent it to a hospital run by nuns. The sisters were delighted. The Kilpatrick's buyer less so.

"Father, if we give you bread, and you then give it away and take away some of our customers, that doesn't work. You can't take away our accounts. The bread is for the Dining Room."

When St. Anthony Farm was in operation, stale bread was hauled to Petaluma, put in the feed mix for the cows and hogs. Another time a whole freight car of macaroni came in, but the Dining Room cooler was completely full. In time, weevils started working on it, so the pasta was hauled to the Farm and put through the mixer for animal feed.

Once a wholesale butcher house gave 2500 steaks. The word spread very quickly, and that day the line got a bit longer than usual. For the Dining Room's forty-fifth anniversary, Hilton Hotels donated prime rib roasts.

Three or four large meat distributors, 20–30 produce firms, four or more bread companies gave food. Pies came from Jack Horner, rice from M.J.B., sugar from Spreckels—all donated. Coffee came from Folger's at wholesale prices. Milk and milk products were donated by Christopher Dairies and Spreckels Russell Dairies.

EARLY DAYS

I don't despair for the human race. Deep down there is a fundamental goodness. Today's crisis period may force the spread of love of one's neighbors, and we really will be brothers to each other.
—Alfred

In the early years the Dining Room operated from one day to the next. It was very poor. A man closely connected with the Dining Room said, "If it wasn't there, it didn't get put in the pot or the oven. Instead of three dishes, there would be two. We had butter once in two years at the Steiner Street residence, where I was living while working at the Dining Room. We had the basics—bread, beans, lamb—morning, noon and night."

The Steiner Street home was for the men working in the kitchen, men who were trying to find their way back. This particular person was a paid employee, but his story is fairly typical of what was happening in the Dining Room.

When all else failed, Father would have Frank Schepergerdes, his right hand man, drive him to the wholesale produce market—the Commission House District—very early in the morning. Alfred in his robe would walk through the stalls, throw his hands up in the air, talking in Italian: "Oh, I need, I need lettuce, beans, cabbage, potatoes . . . ."

"Father, no problem. Come over here."

Frank would drive Father back to the Friary and at 6AM take the truck back to the market and pick up the crates waiting for him. That would feed the Dining Room for the next two or three days.

When the Matson Lines—then carrying passengers to Hawaii and offering Pacific cruises—became interested in the Dining Room, things changed dramatically. As the cruise ships and freighters docked, the crews would clean out the galleys, and all the ship's provisions that were left over went to the Dining Room.

"It was good stuff," Frank declares. "It was a real lifesaver. Before that it was tough."

From the Matson Lines provisions, the Dining Room got butter, margarine, eggs, meat, ham, bacon plus many other things. Now the Dining Room actually got butter!

But the early days *were* tough. People working for the Dining Room would come to Alfred and say, "Father, we need this or that." One man commented that Alfred would look pained and answer, "We don't have the money. We cannot do it. We will have to get it given to us or just do without. We cannot borrow."

Not all the people who wished the Dining Room well would come across and do what they had promised to do. Especially in the early days, Alfred had to learn—often the hard way—which people he could depend on and which he could not. Alfred was warned several times.

"Be careful of so-and-so. They will tell you great things—'Don't worry, Father; I'm going to take care of this for you.' They would then let him hold the bag. Some were prominent people. They made him think they were on his side and then cut him in the back.

'Watch it. You can't rely on them,' he was told." Alfred learned after it happened three or four times. Perhaps they meant well but were people who did not follow through on their promises.

SUPPLIES

*Physical hunger is man's most basic need. When food
is provided, there are deeper hidden hungers to be fed,
along with those of the body.*
—Alfred

So how much food does it take to feed that many
people every day? Lots! For Thanksgiving, to feed 5000
people you start with 335 turkeys, 140 gallons of stuff-
ing, 100 gallons of gravy, 800 pounds of potatoes, 700
pies, 100 gallons of ice cream, 60 pounds of coffee, 800
pounds of yams, plus other vegetables, cranberries and
heaps of salad. Quite a shopping list.

Another breakdown for an average of 2137 daily dinners, which comes to 790,955 meals annually:

Fresh potatoes: 24,000 lbs.

Instant potatoes: 72,000 #10 cans

Rice: 120,000 lbs.

Vegetables: 144,000 lbs.

Bread: 80,000 lbs.; 200 loaves daily

Margarine: 192,000 lbs.

Meat: 408,000 lbs.

Coffee: 4320 lbs.

Sugar: 78,000 lbs.

Milk: 4160 gallons

Dried beans: 450 sacks @ 100 lbs. each

Dried peas: 100 sacks @ 100 lbs. each

When St. Anthony Farm supplied some of the meat the Dining Room needed it was:

One and a half dressed beefs @ 800–900 lbs. each.

Three hogs @ 600 lbs. each.

Three lambs per week @ 300 lbs. each.

Some of this meat was used in the Men's Residence at Seton Hall. Some went to the Madonna Residence. Most of it was used in the Dining Room, cut up for stews, soups and such, plus for gravy and flavoring of the rest of the meals. But the Farm never could produce enough meat to provide everything needed for the Dining Room. Wholesale butcher houses and other donors helped take up the slack.

Yes, this is a long shopping list. But remember there was a long line of hungry people waiting down Golden Gate Avenue believing in the Miracle of Jones Street around the corner.

"We had no soap for laundry," says Frank Schepergerdes of those early days. "We had no soap of any kind. The men at Steiner Street did not have razor blades to shave with."

"I do not have the money," Alfred said.

Then with the help of the sheriff of San Francisco (City and County), Frank went to the local jails once a week to pick up all confiscated blades and razors from the incoming prisoners, so the men who worked in the Dining Room could shave.

In 1955 Adrian Falk was called in to give his opinion how to control and stabilize the food supply. He reported a few days later to the Board of Directors that he had seen the Dining Room and had no idea of the size of the operation. It would take a few more days for him to make an evaluation and decide what was needed.

Falk was an important civic leader, a well-known

philanthropist and the President and Chairman of the Board of S&W Foods of the United States. He had been with that company for some thirty years. He told Alfred he felt he owed the City something. He had not attended college so had worked his way from the bottom up in the organization. He had learned by doing and became Alfred's instructor in private "how to run a business" seminars conducted while Frank Schepergerdes drove Father and Falk around to meet people, establish contacts and order food. Falk was a prominent Jewish leader and became one of Alfred's dearest friends. Through him, Alfred became acquainted with many more of the City's leaders, the movers and shakers who made things go in the City.

Falk arranged to stabilize procurement of food supplies and ordered that any dented cans from the S&W warehouse be sent to the Dining Room. This was another great help to steady the supply of food. It was always critical that there be an even flow. This was the Miracle of Jones Street, and the line was a long one.

Through Falk and Alfred's brother Joe, who worked for the Southern Pacific Railroad Company for many years, Father contacted major farmers, ranchers and growers in the agriculturally rich Central Valley of California, as well as the Salinas-King City area. With introductions to these people, Father and Frank Schepergerdes traveled the length and breadth of California, putting 45,000 miles on the car in two years.

Often Father did not have an introduction. The reference "Him in the brown robe" and his personal touch opened doors to warehouses, homes and offices that could help get the necessary food supplies. In one publication, Father thanked the growers and provisioners in King City, Crows Landing, Modesto, Delano, San Juan

Bautista, Gilroy, Tres Piños, Hollister, San Lucas, San Jose, Sacramento "plus others." That represents a great deal of driving and a great number of contacts.

Many years later, Frank Schepergerdes recalled during an interview: "We went to King City for sugar and beans and all kinds of things—directly to the farmers and ranchers. Father bought soy beans and kidney beans from the growers. He bought feeder hogs from the King City area too and shipped them to Petaluma before the Farm had its own breeding program. He went to the State of Washington and bought a carload of apples once. To Delano for potatoes, to Oregon for lumber for building materials. (Father always needed building materials.)

"In the late '50s we went to see people who lived eight miles east of King City. They were part of the Du Pont family and held a large number of shares in that corporation. As we entered the office, the man was on the phone, saying, 'Okay, 6000 head of feeder cattle tomorrow.' By the time Alfred and I left, Alfred 'had opened the door,' and in a week we had eight head of dressed beef hanging in the San Francisco cooler. From then on we could call—'Ray, we are running short. Can you help us out a little bit?' And a few days later more beef would be hanging in the cooler. Other meat donations were made by Allan Meat Company along with many other wholesale distributors and retailers."

Often, especially in those early days, Father Alfred would go to labor union officials, his neighbors on Golden Gate Avenue near St. Boniface Church. "I need some help. I need to feed all those people you don't employ. You're going to have to do something to help me with this." More he would not say. He had planted the seed. Further he would not go.

In all those many years, the Dining Room never received any financial support from the federal government, the state, the City or the Church. Once someone from the federal government came to Father and told him what he could obtain from its programs. Alfred listened carefully, then said, "I have to think about this. I can't give you an answer right now." And he never did accept the offer. There were never funds from United Crusade, and the Dining Room never got money from the Franciscan Friars either, although they gave great moral support. There was one annual drive plus the pre-Thanksgiving turkey plea. All the money, the food and the provisions came from individuals interested in supporting the Dining Room.

And what do you do with a leftover 218 pound pumpkin? Try donating it to the St. Anthony Dining Room. That is what an Oakland liquor store owner did after he had used the "Great Pumpkin" for a Halloween display. It was delivered at the Dining Room with 5000 Danish pastries, which were welcomed by the guests. There were lots of immediate takers for those. And that pumpkin? First you get it off the truck and into the Dining Room where it decorated the Thanksgiving dinner celebrations, and then it became pies . . . lots of pies.

THE KITCHEN

Food is not enough for the guests at the St. Anthony Dining Room. They must also be treated with courtesy at all times. Many who enter for the first time are uneasy. By welcoming them in a friendly, respectful manner, we can help them escape the feelings of embarrassment.
—Alfred

Cooking for such a number of people is not easy. It has to be well organized and everything run efficiently. Feeding 1500 people in around three hours would strain the resources of any major restaurant. This kitchen had a few paid professionals; the rest were volunteers, so organization had to be topflight. First the salads were made. Most food was prepared in flat pans in the oven or in big pots on the stove. Very little frying was done.

To cook those 335 Thanksgiving turkeys, the work began in July. In the afternoon—after the daily meal had been served and the Dining Room and kitchen were clean—turkeys were roasted in the ovens, then deboned and cut up into serving-size pieces, sealed in plastic bags and frozen. The bones then went into the soup pot for stock. Come the holiday, the frozen bags were put on steamers and the meat came out of the bag hot and fresh. Five thousand turkey dinners takes a bit of planning!

Between 1950 and June 30, 1998, the Dining Room served more than 26.5 million meals.

CLOTHING

*When I donned the robes of St. Francis, I learned
to love every living creature . . . projects squirted
out of my hands. The Dining Room, the Clinic, the
farms, the residence clubs, the foreign students. As
each developed, I have tried to make it self-supporting. There has never been a preset budget or public
relations man. There's been the involvement of thousands of individuals donating time, labor, money,
food stuffs.*

—Alfred

From the very beginning, the need for clothing was
apparent. In the earliest days, clothes were simply given
away. Then a thrift shop was started to earn money to
support the Dining Room. Soon it was clear that clothes
just had to be made available for the people. So clothes
were collected and given away. When Father established
his contacts with the wealthy of the Bay area, many sent
evening gowns and fur coats to the thrift shop. One
person commented, "The gowns were beautiful, worth
thousands and thousands of dollars." Not quite what
was needed in the Tenderloin. It was a simple matter to
sell these furs and gowns to other more upscale thrift
shops and use the funds to buy clothing more appropriate to the area and the needs of the homeless. But
some very resourceful young people did grab the

evening gowns and used the fabric to make drapes for their new apartments.

A humorous incident occurred when a Polk Street boutique was raided for selling the skins of animals and reptiles protected under California's Endangered Species Act. Part of the settlement was that the shoes and boots be donated to St. Anthony's. Thus people in the Tenderloin were seen wearing elegant shoes and boots made of python and kangaroo hides originally intended for a rather upscale—if illegal—market.

Today, clothing and furniture are collected at the Foundation and its warehouse. All kinds of apparel are gladly accepted, but shoes and children's clothes are particularly needed. There is always a line waiting.

THE FIRST FARM

Always positive, optimistic and jovial—very jovial.
Very Franciscan.

> —Beth Payne, Father's secretary for more than 30 years, when asked what Alfred was like.

Father, can you get me outta here? I got to get outta the streets. If I don't, I'll start drinkin' again."

"Help me get out of town, Father."

"If I stay in town, I'll get drunk again, and I'll go right back in the gutter again."

"I would love to get out of town to get my life together again. Please help me."

But there was no place to send them. There was no place to go. It troubled Alfred greatly, but there was nothing he could do. He realized that if some of these men did get out of the Tenderloin and into another environment, maybe they could be helped to help themselves.

Then one day a woman he had never met asked to see Alfred. Her brother had died and left her his half of a small piece of property in Sonoma County. She already owned the other half. They had inherited it from their parents, and neither had children. She told Father that there were five cows and two dozen chickens to be looked after. She hoped that someone from the Dining Room could take care of the place until she could sell the property.

66

Father Alfred remembered, "I went to look at the place, and it occurred to me that I could perhaps use the farm. Perhaps some of the down-and-outers of the Dining Room could restore themselves in such a place. She had been asking $16,000 for the farm, but when I expressed interest, she said, 'If you want it, I'll cut the price in half, and I won't charge you any interest. Pay when you can.'"

Alfred considered carefully. This just might be the answer. So for $8,000, he bought what was called the Vaughn Ranch on Orchard Station Road near Sebastopol. That was 1952. He hoped to send some men there to raise chickens and vegetables for the Dining Room. But things don't always work out just as planned—not even for Father Alfred. The soil was a heavy clay and very rocky, unsuitable for raising very much, and also, water was in very limited supply. So with lemons, one makes lemonade.

"I'm a moral theologian . . . what do I know of farming?" Father asked. But he knew people. If men could get out of the gutter, that would help, but it was not enough. He wanted to get them to work on a farm: to put their hands into the soil and take care of animals—feed them, clean them, nurse them when they were sick. In other words, simply to take responsibility for the care of another living thing. This idea had a long way to go before it could be realized, but it *would* be realized. The Vaughn Place was the first step.

Alfred thought it could all work in several ways. It would get the people off the street—onto a farm—help them straighten out their lives. They in turn could raise hogs, beef, produce—all food for the Dining Room, to help those still *on* the streets.

It was a great idea, but the Vaughn Ranch was not the place, so other uses had to be made of that farm. Wax was collected from used candles or purchased wherever it could be bought cheap. A candlemaking machine was installed, but it required a great deal of water to cool the hot wax, so a one-acre pond was dug. The machine even caught on fire a couple of times. But the men turned out new vigil candles, which were sold at a small profit. Soon there were twenty-nine men at the Vaughn Ranch, and it was bursting at the seams.

ST. ANTHONY FARM

Researchers recognized that this type of life, away from the city, is a most productive way to rehabilitate a person. Farm work, particularly working with animals, seems to help the most.
—Alfred

One day in 1954 Gene Benedetti, who had just been appointed manager of the Cooperative Creamery of Petaluma, got a phone call from Father Alfred. "I'd like to chat with you about some problems we're having."

Gene was a young man at the time, with a growing family. Back from the war—including landing at Normandy on D-Day—he had lost a brother (a Marine aviator) in the Pacific war. He was willing to listen to Father and help if he could.

Gene recalls, "Alfred came to my office in his coarse Franciscan robe, with the thrice-knotted cord symbolizing the Franciscan vows of poverty, chastity and obedience . . . the rosary beads hanging from his belt and Alfred's special touch . . . a few stains and patched elbows."

"I want to build," Alfred told him. "I want a farm to rehabilitate some people. You know a lot of people in the community, Catholics and non-Catholics. I need someplace for these men. A place to keep them busy . . . help them keep their minds off their problems. What I have is too small."

Benedetti asked what he had in mind.

"We have got to get a bigger ranch. We have outgrown the Vaughn Place. We need housing for 40–50 people."

"Father, that's going to cost a lot of money."

"The money will come. The good Lord will take care of it if we can find the right place. I want to see cows, pigs—the men from St. Anthony's can do the work."

Benedetti called in local people who knew the area and had a grasp of the community. A board was formed: John Lounibos, an attorney; John Watson, a prominent farmer, a member of the State Board of Agriculture and a University of California Regent; "Red" Libarle, Earl Dolcini; and, of course, Gene Benedetti, among others.

Benedetti recollects, "We were very concerned about bringing people from the streets into our community. We were a quiet, farming community—very family-oriented, and we wanted no trouble. We went through it thoroughly with Father Alfred. He understood our concerns. There would be strict rules: no drinking, no drugs, no leaving the premises without supervision. The men were to create an atmosphere of caring and getting along with one another. Those rules were strictly enforced. Soon the Farm became known as a place where men were being helped, so that even members of local families would come to the Farm to be cared for. Alfred was right. There were no problems. No one on that ranch ever caused any hassles. Alfred sold us, and I knew he would sell the neighbors, and he sold the guys coming in. No nonsense."

John Lounibos remembered there was a ranch on Two Rock Road that sounded like something Alfred wanted. It was around sixty-three acres. "A nice ranch . . . a husband and wife—Mr. and Mrs. John Messer—want to retire, no children. German people, nice people."

He took Alfred out to see them, and Father struck a deal right away. The agreement was that the Messers would remain living on the property, and the husband was to continue running the operation (there were only six or seven cows). The ranch was valued at around $35,000 . . . fair value for property in 1954.

The men of the Petaluma board were astonished. A quick deal like that was almost unheard-of in rural real estate. They reminded Alfred that the owner had to have a good down payment and the remainder paid out over four to five years.

"Don't worry," Father told them. "The Lord will take care of it. We'll get the money. If I can raise this money, I want to get it. Put up housing. Get it running, get the men in here."

In three weeks they had the money, and the whole thing was signed, sealed and delivered.

"We in Petaluma thought all this was hilarious," Benedetti says. "We country boys had never seen anything that operated like this man operated."

Father told the Messers, "I'm paying for the farm and the house, but I want you and your wife to run it for me. I'm going to bring men from the Dining Room up here. They will have to answer to you for what will have to be done. You tell them what to do. You're on the payroll, too, so you answer to me. Now we want fencing. We want this all cleaned up. Cut the weeds as a start. Then we will start putting up housing for the men from the Vaughn Place and the new men who are coming up from San Francisco."

Alfred brought in Frank Schepergerdes (still manager of the Dining Room but involved with the Farm from the very beginning) and asked: "What is it we really have to do and have here on the Farm to provide for the men and to help the Dining Room?"

"Father, we need to expand and to utilize what we have here. We need cows, a real herd. Possibly hogs. Use what is here. Maybe some feeder steers." Having considered the entire operation carefully, Frank went on. "But first I'm concerned about that creek flooding. I think something needs to be done about that. Then I want to sell milk. I can use the milk money to help support the Dining Room. This will also, in time, give me meat for the Dining Room. And it will give the men who come here work, which is the most important thing."

The creek *was* a problem; in flooding it could cover a good part of the farm. John Watson's son-in-law had a heavy equipment business in the Sacramento Valley, building dams, digging ponds and lakes, leveling land. He brought his men and equipment to the Petaluma farm, dug a pond and leveled the whole landscape. It was a big job and took nearly three weeks, after which, he and his men built a barn. And he never asked for any payment!

Now it was time to get milk cows. Gene Benedetti knew all the dairymen. But the dairy business is—at best—always a very tight operation. To make money, one has to be very careful with expenses and outlay. Gene knew which dairymen would be willing to help, who would not be afraid of being asked to help. Equipped with a list of twenty-six dairymen—many Italian; Italian-Swiss; Portuguese—Father and Frank made the rounds. To Alfred, the doors were opened, and he had his arms outstretched to embrace everyone. The two men went into the homes, into the kitchens, of people Alfred had never seen before in his life. He would soon be sitting in a chair, have his arm around someone, playing with the children, speaking

Italian or a little Portuguese. Usually he had the promise of cow or a calf—a Holstein, the black-and-white ones Gene said were best. In some instances Alfred had the promise of a calf a year for replacement stock.

"Frank, go pick them up Tuesday," Alfred would say. Frank soon had twenty-two milking cows. Very quickly that figure jumped to 60–70 milkers.

Much to the amusement of the local dairymen, Father was nonplussed when he was told he would get some springers. So what in the world was a springer . . . a jumper? Why would a cow jump?

"No, Father, a springer is a heifer that is springing."

"Oh?"

"Going to have a calf."

"Why the expression?"

"Who knows?"

Soon Father could talk about springers with the best of the dairymen. And so the moral theologian became a dairy farmer!

When the housing was in place, men came to St. Anthony Farm. But the whole thing got to be too much for the Messers. Alfred needed a new farm manager, and Frank Schepergerdes decided he wanted to be at the Farm full time.

FRANK SCHEPERGERDES

"Visualize, organize, deputize and supervise."
—A sign over Alfred's desk

Not seeing the future he wanted in what he was doing at the Dining Room, Frank Schepergerdes told Alfred, "Either I go to the Farm or I go to another area."

Father did not want to lose Frank from the San Francisco operation—"not in the worst way."

"I was raised on a farm." Frank explained recently. "And to be with street people the rest of my life, that was not what I came to America for. I lived with them on Steiner Street, ate with them seven days a week for almost three years. It was the experience of my life. But the Dining Room was not my future. I had a wife and children now. I went to the Farm and for five years traveled back and forth from Petaluma to San Francisco. And that was before Highway 101 was a freeway. You had to go through all the towns then and stop for all the stoplights. And I was trying to build up the Farm and still help with all the things going on in the Dining Room."

For Frank the Farm was back where he belonged. As a young boy in Northern Germany during World War II, he had done most of the farm work. The men of the family had been drafted into the Wehrmacht and were on the Russian front; most did not return. His boyhood experience gave Frank a diverse knowledge of animals, crops, machinery and the problems involved in organizing day-to-day farm operations. The several years he worked as the manager of the Dining Room had honed his administrative skills as well as giving him expertise in dealing with men who had simply forgotten how to function in society. Now these men needed to learn to work again and to organize time and effort. Frank would teach them.

Dozens of blackboards were tacked on the walls of the swine and dairy barns, the feed mill and the other buildings. Scrawled on these boards were instructions for each job, just in case the men forgot how something was to be done or the exact time they were supposed to do it. "I think we [had] more blackboards than all the schools in Sonoma County," joked Frank Schepergerdes.

Learning to work and function again was crucial for these men. It was their passport for re-entry into society. Also important was that they relearn society's rules. They had to agree to the rules of the Farm. Without that the operation could not coexist with a quiet rural community. Local people needed to be reassured that what was happening at the Farm was what was promised by Father Alfred. The entire success of the rehabilitation program and the Farm depended on it.

A professional milker was hired. In time the milking herd would number 170–180 cows, plus calves, springers and dry stock (cows not being milked, either because they were too old or were awaiting a calf) for a total of around 400 head of stock. But most of the work of the Farm would be done by the men who had come from the streets of San Francisco.

"Working with animals is therapeutic," said Frank. "The livestock often provided the affection that is missing from these men's lives. Sometimes the animals build the bridge to a real life. They are always there, ask for nothing and give everything."

FARM WORK

You should have seen some of the guys who came up here," Gene Benedetti says, "and some were smart people. They were real rough types. After a couple of weeks, they were clean-shaven. Hair cut. Alfred had a code: No one went off the Farm unless they had the authority to do it. No one did. It was amazing.

"When Father Alfred got behind a thing, it went. It was automatic. You couldn't say no to the man, and you didn't want to say no. He could sell iceboxes to Eskimos. I never saw anyone like him. Pure goodness just flowed out of him. He always got the things he needed. It was amazing. People were willing to give to him because they knew it was for a good cause. Everyone loved him. The women who formed the auxiliary, they loved him. Kids . . . everyone.

"Alfred would pick our brains clean, and he would tell us what he was doing. The only thing he didn't tell us was where he got the money. The payroll was small—Frank, milkers and a couple of men. The Farm was not a model farm in the sense of labor efficiency. It was not intended to be."

Frank Schepergerdes explains, "Our number one product was the men. The dairy and hog operation was brought in to create work, make jobs and—at the same time—to bear the expenses of the rehabilitation."

The forty men, on average, who resided at the Farm rose at 6AM and worked around forty hours per week, each

77

to his ability, his talent and his strength. There were jobs in the dormitory; cook, dishwasher, houseman. There were gardeners for the extensive gardens providing fresh, wholesome vegetables for the farm table. Barn jobs included washing the cows before they were milked, feeding the cows, constantly cleaning the milking area and washing and sterilizing the milking equipment. This was a very important job, one on which the whole milking department depended. The calf barn required men to feed, clean, and care for the calves. The hospital barn needed men who—with love and care—looked after the sick animals and worked with veterinarians. In addition, there were cows, heifers and dry stock to be fed and cared for. On a farm or ranch, there is never a lack of things to do.

Feed had to be mixed. In the early days it was purchased, but to cut costs and to create jobs, a mill was bought, and the Farm mixed its own feed. In addition to cutting costs and providing jobs, this operation could utilize foods that otherwise might be wasted—for example, that stale bread and pasta. One attempt was made to use vegetables and fruits near spoiling, but Frank said he vetoed the idea. There too many problems involved, and it simply did not work.

Other skills needed were carpentry (something always needs building or fixing on a farm of that size), painting, fence-building, machinery operation and repairs. Even mixing and pouring of concrete has to be understood. Men could update old skills and learn new ones to take into the job market. The manager's house was built by the men of the Farm. The dormitory later was largely constructed by the men themselves.

Father's faith—that working with animals and the soil was a positive force that could help men overcome their problems—was being justified. Men were returning to real life. After they left St. Anthony Farm, the men could go to Covenant House, a San Francisco residential facility for recovering alcoholics and addicts that provided free housing, support and counseling while they looked for and obtained jobs. Frank's recommendations carried great weight with prospective employers. After six months, the men moved out on their own but still could get counseling and help. A good percentage were able to stay clean, to get jobs, to rebuild their lives, to rejoin their families. Some did return to the Farm, and some disappeared and were never heard from again.

Teresa Boeddeker, Father's sister-in-law observed, "It was so wonderful to take men out of the gutter, put them in clean clothes, provide a real bed, give them three good meals per day, and they worked hard. They were away from drinking and drugs. They could smoke. They enjoyed each other's company. They were living again. Living a normal life. Their self-image and their bodies improved. They were producing something which made them feel good.

"It was interesting to see how some of these guys came back to life. Many were so far down in the dumps, they would tell you, 'I don't think I'll ever get out. I'll just hang on till it's over—till I die.'

"After a while they got a little bit of spark, started to bounce back. Some of the boys who came back, got in touch with their mothers and fathers. It was beautiful. What a wonderful reunion."

A small sign on the wall of the Dining Room informed newcomers that there was further help . . . clothing, shelter, medical and nursing care, employment opportunities and a stay at St. Anthony Farm. In 1995, the Foundation announced that nine thousand people had taken part in its drug and alcohol rehabilitation program.

HOGS

The humble hog got us over the hump.
　　　　　　—Alfred

*It was the hog operation that put the Farm on a se-
cure financial basis, so that we could provide for the
men, our real product.*
　　　　　　—Frank Schepergerdes

Alfred decided the Farm should raise hogs on a large
scale. Swine take relatively little space, compared to
sheep or cows. They are fairly labor-intensive and can
utilize a great deal of waste dairy products. "Think Big"
was Alfred's motto. In keeping with this, he sent Frank
to the Midwest and Europe to study the latest methods
of swine production. Returning with some clear ideas
of what was needed, Frank designed and built hog pens
that were efficient, yet still required a good deal of labor so the men would have work.

A flush system of sanitation was installed to separate
the solid from the liquid waste, the former eventually
was sold as dry fertilizer and the latter held in the lagoons for later spreading onto the pasture land through
sprinkler irrigation. But it was still necessary to hand-
clean the pens and stalls, for the work itself was part of
the rehabilitation.

One all-important feature was to design farrowing

(birthing) stalls that were the newest in the industry. A major problem in the swine business is losing piglets when a sow rolls onto her babies. This was solved by a design making such an event almost impossible. Yet men remained with the sows on a 24-hour basis, making the rounds of the farrowing pens to help the sows with the births . . . midwiving pigs! Frank said he would often catch sight of a man picking up a piglet, stroking it, and even kissing it when he thought no one was looking. The Farm had around 18 boars to 400 sows, with a total of 3800 hogs in a farrow-to-finish operation.

The dairy also needed a great deal of modern equipment: milking machines, a milking parlor, stainless steel cabinets for milk and holding tanks. These were bought and installed so that the Farm could sell Grade A milk. Father was a great believer in making things stand on their own without further need of donations to keep them going. Later the Farm ran on a budget of close to $1 million. It became a medium-sized dairy selling milk. Yet always the major product was the men and their rehabilitation.

Again Frank commented, "Often the media would ask Father, 'How much money is the Farm making?' He would never tell them that. His only answer was 'God is good.'"

An important aspect of the dairy business is that there is a very high volume of spoilage—in milk, cream, cottage cheese and sour cream. Bay Area dairies such as Spreckels Russell, Berkeley Farms, and Golden State (later Foremost), gave Alfred returned dairy products past their shelf life. Men from the Farm drove to the City, picked up the returned items, which were then dumped into large tanks on the Farm and mixed with grain for hog swill. Lots and lots of milk went into those hogs.

A surprising problem occurred during cold weather, when bacteria formed in the milk and killed a number of pigs. It took a bit of doing to find the cause. Bacteria built up in pasteurized and homogenized milk. Normally in untreated milk this does not happen. The solution was to put electric rods into the milk storage tanks to keep the milk at a constant temperature of 80 degrees. At that temperature the bacteria would not form and the swill would be ready to feed the swine.

The Farm at one time operated around 1000 acres, most of it leased. Corn was raised for silage, which is fermented corn and excellent feed for dairy cows. The silage operation was a very successful one. It cut down the consumption of hay, which had to be bought and could be extremely expensive from time to time.

One of many Farm success stories started out tragically. A construction worker lost his wife and daughter when a teenager high on cocaine and liquor smashed his car into them at 75 mph. The man lost his family; then he lost his job and finally, his home. Lastly he became a drug addict, calling himself a dope fiend. "St. Anthony Farm was my last hope," he said later. He was one who made it back.

THE ENVIRONMENT

I never ask. I tell them what I would like to do, and if they think it is a good deal, they'll help me. I've never said "can you help me with this." I don't have to ask. It comes to me as fast as I need it.
—Alfred

In the late 1960s and early 1970s came problems with pollution and concerns for the environment. New regulations stated farms could not have runoff sewage (manure) going into a creek. All local dairymen had to comply, and the North Coast Water Quality Control Board was pushing St. Anthony Farm to comply as well.

Gene Benedetti describes the problem and how it was handled: "We kept stalling. With our expansion, the dam could no longer hold all the water that we were flushing into the pond . . . washing the cows, the dairy equipment, washing down the stalls, and then the same thing for the hogs. The officials held off as long as they could. The Farm was a charity, but finally the word came.

" 'We can't delay any longer. You will have to comply.'

" 'Okay, would you talk to Alfred? Tell him the same story you told me.'

" 'Okay.'

"We had lunch at Frank's house. [Greta, Frank's wife and Father's cousin, was great at making lunches for all who came to the Farm. She even kept records of what was served to whom.] Alfred came up from San Francisco. The officials gave the Farm one year to meet all the new regulations. It would have to have [an upgraded] milking parlor and build lagoons to hold the effluence. The estimated cost was $200,000 or better.

"Alfred's only comment was, 'Let me give this some thought. I'll call you in a week and let you know what I think. I want to keep the dairy. It is great for the men.'

"I got the call, 'Gene, could you come down next week? I need to make a presentation to about twelve people about the ranch. Come down and support me. Bring Frank. You tell them what's needed and why.' Father was bang-bang-let's go when he had made up his mind to do something.

"The lunch was at the Fairmont Hotel in Ben Swig's private suite on the top floor. It was very grand with a magnificent view of the entire Bay. And a table set for fifteen people. It was something else again. Very elegant. Father introduced us to everyone. We ate a marvelous lunch, and I made the presentation: what the problem was, why it was critical. Frank then spoke to the group and showed some pertinent slides. Alfred said, 'Now look. I think this is a very necessary part of our program—to the kitchen and to get people out of the streets. There has been no cost to any public agency in all this. We have had a great rehabilitation success rate. I'd like a decision on this. I have a time limit. This has to be done on such-and-such a date. I've got to have commitments.'

"Alfred got $190,000 that day, with the promise that the group would get the rest 'when you need it. Let us know.' The checks written were for $10,000–$15,000 per person!"

Later Alfred said, "These are kind people. Everything I've done, they have been a part of."

Benedetti says, "They loved him. You could see it. They loved him. He just said 'this is what is needed,' and they helped. This luncheon I went to was amazing. I never saw anything like it. I couldn't believe it. 'This is what has to be done. I leave it to you.' And these people did it."

"Alfred cut across all social lines in the City," Frank Schepergerdes points out. "Ben Swig was one of his best friends. Adrian Falk couldn't say enough good about Alfred. And couldn't back him enough."

Frank then spent several months studying water pollution systems on other California dairies. He laid out the plans for the system that was needed, and the men of the Farm did the construction. Lagoons were installed to collect and hold the effluence from the dairy and hog pens. A manure separator took out the solids, and the environmental problem was solved to everyone's satisfaction.

"St. Anthony Farm is one of the most innovative farm operations in the country," reported the *Press Democrat* of Santa Rosa.

While the major product of the Farm was the men, it *did* supply some meat and other food for the Dining Room. Meat was always the big problem for "Tony's Place." It was expensive, and donations were precarious, depending on the goodwill of people like in King City. Other times wholesalers who donated could go out of business.

On the Farm the old Holsteins were slaughtered. This was a surer, steadier source of supply but did not come close to providing all the meat the Dining Room needed; yet it was an important part of the whole. Frank had learned to slaughter and butcher when he was growing up in Germany. In Petaluma he taught the men these skills. The Farm never had a professional butcher. All the equipment was there: a cooler to age the meat, the proper knives, the necessary butcher blocks, equipment to hang the meat, freezers to store it. Frank and the men did it all: slaughtered, cut up the meat, wrapped it and put it in the freezer.

The farrow-to-finish operation of the hogs meant the pigs were fed for 5–5½ months. Every ten days a truck and trailer rig from the slaughterhouse pulled into the Farm and hauled away 200 swine. Such animals averaged 240 pounds each, and the Farm raised around 8000 hogs per year for sale. This was what kept the Farm going, made it pay for itself so that the men had work and a home and could get their lives back together again.

RITA

No one sends these men, not the courts, not the police nor a priest. They just want to get off the streets.
—Frank Schepergerdes

The men were off the street, had a nice room, an address, a telephone to contact their families, a shave, a haircut, clean clothes and a good night's sleep. It worked wonders on many. Many made it, but not all. After all, this is a true story.

Rita Schepergerdes, Frank and Greta's daughter who was raised on the Farm, tells another part of the story: "I walked up and down the lane as a little girl. I lived on the Farm for eighteen years. I came in constant contact with the men who lived there. At first, growing up with derelicts didn't even occur to me as a problem. I told people at school about the Farm and I'd get questions. Oh, gosh. I had always been treated with the utmost respect and politeness and consideration by anyone I encountered. There was always a mutual respect, a dignity thing. People would say to me, 'That's the last sort of thing you would expect from *that* sort of person.'

"Ridiculous! Looking back, I grew up in a house built by homeless people—one of whom was a surveyor for the county for twenty years. Over and over, basic civility aside, all the people had their particular skill or gift or talent or whatever ability. And the people who are so often discounted as worthless or having nothing to offer to society, could make a substantial contribution if anyone would give them the time of day, acknowledge them as a person . . . they had something to offer. It is easier, almost, to think of them as people you can throw away. Because then you don't owe them anything. Throwaway people. But to acknowledge that they have a real contribution and their dignity is worth something means you have to enter into a mutual debt. That's where a lot of social workers stop. People's attitude toward the homeless stops, because they don't want to enter into that.

"The Farm did. Father Alfred assured the Petaluma people it was going to work and it did! How did it work? So much depended on the sense of dignity which was so important to Father Alfred. If you believe the best in someone else or give them an indication that you expect something good of them, they are so much more likely to show that side of themselves to you.

"But if you are condescending or say, 'Try not to cause trouble while you are here.' If that's what you put in the forefront . . . 'You shape up while you are here.' You don't get the best out of people that way. But if you approach them as he did, with leaving the door open to the good in them—especially when they haven't been approached by anyone that way in a long time—they are ready to give that and open up that part of themselves.

"You drive up to this impressive farm. We entertained certain important people in our home: religious people, community people and media people. Mom would serve up meals upon meals. Oh, it was all so impressive. The Farm was running well, and it seemed there was this big mystery. How could this happen? How could it run so smoothly? Of course some of that was management but the other was the abilities and the goodness in the people who are there and their willingness to do as they were told. I think sometimes people shut off, and it all becomes a big mystery. How does it function? When the people who are holding up their end—the residents that is—they do have something to offer, and I think people don't want to acknowledge that."

THE AUXILIARY

*No attempt was made at rehabilitation. There were
no social workers, no psychologists. Nothing was said
or done overtly; the only therapy that was performed
was by decent surroundings, fresh air, good food, com-
panionship, hard work and contact with Mother Earth.
These things do the healing. The men thus aided to
restore themselves.*
                    —Alfred

The Farm Auxiliary is an organization of local Sonoma
and Marin County women willing and able to help with
the Farm. It was they who could and would give the
dormitory a homelike atmosphere: such touches as bed-
spreads and curtains in the bedrooms, slipcovers on the
chairs, drapes, pictures on the wall and flowers on the
table—all of which had been missing in the utilitarian
male world of the Farm.

The Auxiliary even procured trees and shrubs to make
the buildings look less institutional. One year they provided an iron and an ironing board, plus thermal blankets and new pillows for forty beds. The men needed
farm boots when they arrived. Most had street shoes
unsuitable for farm work (if they had shoes at all). Also
they needed slippers for house wear to feel relaxed in
the evenings. The Auxiliary helped to supply such
things.

For holidays such as Easter, Thanksgiving or Christmas the members made special decorations and planned parties. Their goal was to make this farm as much as possible a home, the home these men had lost. On such feast days, the members provided a menu requested by the men. Music, a tree, refreshments and gifts at Christmas were an important part of theAuxiliary's activities. The Christmas party was perhaps the most touching of all. The singing of carols united all, though some were so touched they could only sing in their hearts . . . or were hurting from so long an absence of such joy that they could only feel and not say aloud. Father would always give a brief warm talk.

The Auxiliary, which finally numbered 240–250 members, worked hard to make the men of the Farm feel they mattered, that people cared about them, that they had a real home and, of course, that they had dignity.

Farm Day in June—sponsored by the Auxiliary—was a big event, with an open house and a chicken barbecue. Food, live music and a guided tour of the Farm by the residents were part of the program. Well-known beyond Sonoma County, it drew visitors by the hundreds. Father always enjoyed the big crowd; it gave him an added opportunity to meet and thank people for their help and support. (Farm Day is still celebrated each June.)

The Spring Luncheon was Father's treat for the ladies. He always recognized people who helped and worked in the various organizations. Women involved from the beginning included: Mickey Dolcinci, Millie Libarle and Madalyn Toohey, among many others.

Typical of the support the Farm enjoyed from the community, a local dentist—without publicity—provided his services to the men for several years, seeing to it that they had good dental care.

THE MEN OF THE FARM

Alfred had a way that anything he said was very important.
            —Father John Vaughn

I mean I was close to dyin' of that stuff I'd been drinking," admitted Joe, a former X ray technician. He was shaking and feeling his stomach was about to cave in that day in February when he chose to hop the Farm truck. Later, Joe said of the Farm, "Now this ain't no paradise, but I'm doing a lot better."

Another graduate of the Farm told the press, "Six months of the Farm saved my life. I learned that I am not a bum, that I'm just an addict. I can give something back. And I want to."

A man who had disappeared twenty-two years before was welcomed home by his son, a Washington State automobile dealer. Having heard of his father's stay at the Farm, he came to pick him up and take him home.

A 17-year-old runaway from Alabama came to the Farm almost afraid to talk to anyone. Working there, he learned to accept and carry out responsibilities. He left the Farm with a good recommendation and was last heard from working as the foreman on a large Idaho cattle ranch.

A towering man known as Mike O'Reilly, after a time at the Farm, quickly worked himself up to be a respected and trustworthy houseman at St. Anthony Dining Room. Only after he had died of cancer did his real identity papers indicate that he was a former court reporter from a very wealthy San Francisco family. Somewhere he took a wrong turn and then the right turn—to the Farm. He had taken another name with his new life. At his funeral his sister said to Alfred, "Where Dick lost, Mike won."

Many things contributed to the men's problems: a marriage breakup or the loss of a spouse. Some moved from elsewhere and could not find a job. Or it was a drinking problem and/or more recently, a drug problem. For kids maybe it was rebellion, maybe just not fitting in, maybe abuse in the home or a badly dysfunctional family.

The men were asked three questions when they came to the Farm:

Name? Whom to notify in case of an accident? What kind of work did you do before?

There were two rules:

You can leave anytime, but you can't leave and come back in a few days. Absolutely no drinking or drugs.

"The Dining Room guys were good guys, really nice men," Frank Boeddeker recalled. Of one he said: "He was a particularly good worker, a decent guy. He was working for me. One day he told me 'I'd like to be back home again . . . Detroit, that's where I'm from. I'd like to get back together with my wife. I hear from her once in awhile. But I don't have enough money.' I told him, 'Okay, you help me finish this building and I'll help you.' I got him on a bus to Detroit. He got together with his wife. He made it. Got a job. I heard from him for a few years and then lost track. But he made it.

"But recovering from alcoholism or drug addiction

is not easy. Sometimes the men work for a time. All goes well. 'Hey, I could get paid for this' and off they would go. Sometimes they came back to try again. Sometimes not. No one can win 100 percent of the time."

Life on the Farm was not easy. Maintenance and care of the animals were demanding tasks which had to be done every day. The Farm was known for its strong emphasis on cleanliness, which meant that a lot of manure had to be shoveled. Every man was free to leave when he chose, but encouraged to work while he was there. The average stay was thirty-eight days ... some stayed less time, others more, some stayed on for years. No one was questioned about his past or was preached to while on the Farm. There was no question as to color or creed.

One who had been in other programs said, "St. Anthony's is different. You are left alone to work out your problems. You are expected to put in a hard day's work but the treatment is just and fair, and the food is very good. And we are treated with respect."

Father was convinced that country life with hard work, less stress and—most of all—contact with animals and the earth was the great healer. His faith is borne out in the following story from one man on the Farm:

"Last April, I helped deliver a calf. It was the first time I had experienced a birth of any kind. The calf was premature and so weak she couldn't stand. No one expected her to live. She was on straw in the corner of the stall. She couldn't nurse because she couldn't stand. All I could think of was that I wanted to see her live. Some of us decided to pull her through. We took turns nursing her, giving her bottles of milk, covering her with a blanket, rubbing her and sitting with her.

"It paid off. She began to gain weight and strength. She got to her feet and took a few steps and started to suck. In a couple of years she will be producing milk here on the Farm like all the rest of the cows. We're a lot alike. I'm taking some awkward steps. I came to St. Anthony's after I realized I wasn't going to make it. I had lost my job, was thrown out of my place, and doing dope all the time. I knew I had to get clean."

Another Farm story—there are so many—tells of a man who had been going down for thirteen years when he found the Farm. "I think I can make it back now. I hope even to have a family again."

His was a particularly poignant tale. He had been a highly successful fashion photographer with a home, a wife and five young children. On returning from an assignment in Europe just before Christmas, he found his house had burned to the ground and his entire family was dead in the ruins. He cracked. He went on a drunken binge from New York to San Francisco, where he woke up in the gutter near St. Anthony Dining Room. From there he went to the Farm. After slopping hogs for a while, he made it back.

"They really treat you decent. They have a lot to offer here. I'm learning a lot of trades and they give you a job recommendation when you're ready to leave."

THE NEW DORMITORY

It's not fair to call them bums. Everything you see here has been built by the men.
—Alfred

In 1970 a dream came true for Father Alfred. A new residence hall for the Farm was completed and dedicated. The men had been living in two residence halls, too small for the number of men and not comfortable enough to suit Father. A local architect drew up the plans for a flat fee. A contractor did the basic work and built the shell. From there on, the Farm men—with Frank as the supervisor—did all the finishing work: the heating, plumbing and electrical work; putting up the walls and finishing and painting them; everything except laying the carpets.

The hall is a spacious 11,000 square feet. It has a large entry which was used for various meetings—such as the Farm Board—a lunchroom near the kitchen, a large dining room adjoining that with a wonderful view of the valley and nearby hills, two television rooms and sleeping rooms for the forty men.

Father Alfred commented once, "I look on each one who comes to us as my brother. I could be in that line if things had turned out differently." His listeners seemed surprised by this observation.

The Vaughn Ranch remained part of the St. Anthony property. It raised Christmas trees when the men transferred to the Messer Farm. Later, Alfred opened it to Dominican contemplative nuns whose New York convent had literally crumbled under them, leaving them nowhere to go.

They now lived a hermit life on the Vaughn Ranch (presently called the Hermitage) with chickens, cats, a dog and wild ducks on the pond. Alfred often went there to say Mass in their lovely chapel. He would sit, watch the clouds, enjoy the grass, the trees and those ducks swimming on the pond. And he would relax—out of the Tenderloin.

"Alfred was a man of tremendous vision and one of the most spiritual people I have ever known." Thus Sister Mike (Michael) of the Vaughn Ranch summed him up.

POOR CLARES

*If the Lord wants it, He will find a way. Don't worry
about the money.*
                    —Alfred

In the very early 1950s, the Poor Clares—a cloistered,
contemplative religious order established by St. Francis
and St. Clare—lost their house in the Fruitvale section
of Oakland. Alfred offered to help them. The parents of
one of the nuns had given the Order a ten-acre lot in
Santa Cruz, and they had $25,000 in cash resources. To
Alfred's question, did they want a convent on the Santa
Cruz property the answer was *Yes.* "Well, we'll take care
of that," Alfred said and set out to help them build a
new convent.

An architect volunteered to design the building,
which was no easy task. Under the rules of the Order at
that time, once a woman had entered the convent, she
could not leave. That meant that the convent had to have
hospital facilities, even be prepared for surgery, plus a
dental office. It needed a chapel for the nuns "inside"
plus a church on the "outside" so local people could
worship there too. It even had to have its own cemetery,
because the nuns must be buried within the convent
walls.

When the bids came back, they were for a whopping
$600,000. Thus Serra Construction Company was born.

Who was Serra Construction? Why, Father Alfred, of course—Father Alfred and friends. The whole convent construction project would take nearly two years.

"I never saw anything like it," brother Frank Boeddeker declares. "Somehow Father had just enough to make each payroll. One week he would pay the lumber bill; the next week the workers would get their checks. Men from the Dining Room came down. Some were quite skilled; some wanted to learn. I did a lot of the work and hired local union workers. Goodman Lumber Company gave enough fence material, shim stock [the first cut of lumber at the edge of the log] to build a fence ten feet high around the ten-acre lot. That was the first thing we put up.

"One of the nuns had a close connection with Goodman's. She was either a daughter or a niece and said that company would give a hand in the construction.

"There were some real problems. The engineer and the architect did not get along. Didn't talk to each other. So the support columns which should have been inside the walls were out in the middle of the rooms. We covered them and then marbleized them, and they really looked beautiful.

"When it was finished and Mother Abbot came to operate the convent, everything was first-rate. The final cost was $200,000. Unfortunately, later the State of California bought the site for an off ramp for a freeway. And the nuns had to move again."

Frank also told how he and Father often stopped by to see the nuns, who prepared lunch for them. "Always tuna sandwiches. Never anything else." Frank often wondered if that was all they had to eat.

THE CLINIC

To be sick in addition to being poor and hungry is intolerable.
                                                —Alfred

T.B. doesn't bother them. It kills them, but it doesn't bother them," said Dr. Francis Curry of the San Francisco Department of Public Health after viewing the first-aid station at St. Anthony's in 1957. "More important, they all have lice, many have scabies, and all have sores on their feet and legs. Your first-aid clinic is totally inadequate. You have lots of samples all mixed up." His blunt advice to Alfred? "Throw everything out and start over. Get a real clinic."

"Okay. How much will it cost?"

Dr. Curry had come to Father proposing to deal with the tuberculosis problem in the Tenderloin, Alfred's parish. "Well, for the rest of this year $40,000 and then $80,000 per year."

Father Alfred almost fainted. At that time the biggest pockets of tuberculosis in the United States were in the downtown slum areas of major cities.

But the Dining Room was already running on a "touch-and-go" basis. It was costing around $100 per day to operate in 1957 dollars, and at the end of the year there might be $3000 left over. Might be. Every day was "let's see if we can make it." There was no $40,000—

much less $80,000—for *anything*. There was barely enough to keep the Dining Room open.

Alfred had long been aware of the untreated health problems of his guests. Some were so seriously ill that they had been referred to San Francisco General Hospital for immediate admission and treatment. He had established, next to the Dining Room, a small triage and first-aid station so that minor medical problems could be treated immediately on the premises. A few physicians and nurses from St. Joseph's Hospital volunteered their services a few hours each week. The most common infections were colds, sinusitis and sore throats. Gastroenteritis and skin infections and infestations of lice were also common.

Now Dr. Curry wanted to throw out the first-aid station, x-ray the people in the line, clean up tuberculosis and then set up a "real clinic" under the auspices of the St. Anthony Dining Room—for $40,000 Alfred did not have. Another very serious consideration was that if publicity came out about the tuberculosis problem, there might be repercussions.

"Oh, no! If we run T.B. testing through here, the City will close us down. Most of these men come from South of Market. Canon Kip House of the Episcopal Church has a mission there with a retired army colonel in charge. It is their area."

Canon Kip House said, "It is a wonderful idea but 'no.' Go north of Market."

Back to Alfred. "You have to."

So, of course he did. In 1958, the Tuberculosis Control Division of the San Francisco Health Department asked to use the Clinic area three mornings a week from eight to eleven. They wished to demonstrate that tuberculosis could be treated effectively out-of-hospital in an urban core neighborhood, without danger to the general public and with good patient compliance.

"We couldn't change their lifestyle." Dr. Curry explained in an interview many years later. "We merely got in their way each day by locating next door [to the Dining Room]. We had public health nurses hauling them off the food line. They were given a card that would later let them go to the head of the line. So, if anything, that probably motivated them."

As a result of the treatment program, there was a great drop in the hospitalization rate of tuberculosis sufferers, and this dread disease was shown to be controllable. The number of infected people dropped, as did the cost of treating them. This pleased the City. The success of this project was recognized by the National Tuberculosis Association as a landmark study and served as the basis for modern ambulatory outpatient treatment of tuberculosis.

The Clinic then was organized to provide limited general medical care to the Tenderloin and the South of Market area. Until 1977 this was the only free medical service in the area. Doctors and nurses contributed their time and skills. The patients were very cheerful and cooperative; they knew something was being done for them. Dr. Curry stated that there was only one violent incident that he recalled when one patient waiting in line murdered another by cutting his throat. Shocking enough but—considering the number of clients and their problems—not that surprising.

Policy statement Number One of the Clinic: "No barbiturates, no tranquilizers, no narcotics shall be prescribed, dispensed, stocked or stored. None of these drugs shall be on hand. Any patient requiring such shall be referred to other appropriate medical care. Only over-the-counter drugs are dispensed."

Many of the health problems of the men and women of the area were caused by the simple fact that they had no shoes. Not having shoes is not a simple matter to the person on the street. Working people, middle America, may complain that shoes wear out too fast, but they can be replaced. Not easy for someone who is down and out. The U.S. Rubber Company in San Francisco had piles of mismatched shoes, which they simply threw away. The problem was put to the company, and they forwarded these unsaleable shoes to St. Anthony's to give away. They might only last a few months, but the people could then get another pair. The feet and legs of the recipients improved dramatically.

Alfred was astonished. "We help the hungry; now we help to clothe them, and we drastically reduce foot diseases by getting them shoes!"

Years later, speaking of the early days of the Clinic, Dr. Curry said, "The hardest part I had putting it all together was getting people here who are truly professional, who could practice their art and science without being judgmental about their patients' lives or feel these people are human garbage. Their clothes are filthy, their skin dirty, their odors rough, because they have no place to take a bath. They have lice, scabies, skin infections from scratching. We're [the staff] conscious of it but push it aside and see beyond the skin and odor to the real human dignity, no matter how badly they've been crushed. And they respond beautifully."

In the first three months, the Clinic saw around a hundred people per day, five days a week. Hospitalization, when needed, was provided by Presbyterian Hospital, St. Mary's Hospital and San Francisco General. Doctors and nurses from those institutions volunteered their time and skills. Resident physicians were also assigned to provide services. For many years, there were very few salaried staff members at the Clinic. In 1982 the total yearly budget of the Clinic was approximately $128,000 for around 15,000 patients. That averaged around $20 per visit.

Another health and sanitation problem was the lack of public showers and public toilets in the Tenderloin. In the Main Library, a few blocks from St. Anthony's, the Men's Room was a favorite place for street people to wash. They would strip naked and wash themselves. Men studying at the library were startled to enter the men's room and find a street person stark-naked trying to wash himself. He would then put his dirty clothes back on, lice and all.

Around 1960 a local television station ran a special on the Clinic that was starting up and what its needs would be. Charles Kuralt picked up the story and gave it national attention, calling it " . . . from a medical standpoint, the best program that I knew of . . . ."

The next morning an 80-year-old lady from the top of Nob Hill, a dear friend of Father Alfred's, came to the Clinic office. She was riding in her new Rolls Royce and wearing an elegant wide-brimmed hat with a pink ribbon, Dr. Curry remembered. "Some things you don't forget. I can still see that pink ribbon on that hat." He would not divulge her name. "I'm still not at liberty to say." She was certainly in marked contrast to the Tenderloin scene.

"I heard about the Clinic," she said. "Take me around to see it."

"It is not really on public exhibition," was Dr. Curry's first response.

But of course, she was shown the Clinic. She talked to the patients, asked what was going on and was apprised of what was needed.

"Take me to the office, please."

There she wrote out a check.

Dr. Curry took a deep breath, "I need more than that."

She wrote another check. The second for $10,000 to go with the first for $28,000.

"I was dumbfounded . . . stunned," says Dr. Curry.

Alfred was overwhelmed and said to Curry simply, "You go get the things needed."

That contribution got things going. Improvements in the Clinic, showers, toilets, washing machines to clean the clothes and dryers to dry them.

Recently in an annual report, the Bethesda Program (as it is now known)—right next to the Clinic— provided 18,000 showers, 3300 haircuts, 6000 laundry washings to street people who had no other place to get clean. In addition nearly 400 people got direct counseling.

"Many of the people had been on the streets for so long and were so dirty, that they were despondent. Now here was a chance," Dr. Curry remembered with a great deal of emotion.

The Bethesda Program also provides mailboxes. Without an address, people cannot receive mail (and cannot apply for many social services), so the homeless are cut off from vital resources. With these mailboxes they can receive personal mail and checks, such as pension checks, social security checks, and whatever else they are entitled to.

With the great influx of the boat people—refugees from Southeast Asia—in the 1970s, the needs of the Clinic changed again. Families from Vietnam, Cambodia and Laos were being settled in the Tenderloin. Translators were needed and doctors speaking the necessary languages. Generally, the Southeast Asian mothers and children came to the Clinic but the men were afraid at first. Now the Southeast Asians are becoming a potent force in the area and are creating a real neighborhood.

"The neighborhood had some pretty tough characters," Dr. Curry said with a bit of a smile.

Yet neither Father Alfred nor any Franciscan was ever threatened in any way in or near the Dining Room or the Clinic. But once a very tall ex-basketball player came up to Dr. Curry. "Little man, come here."

Dr. Curry was possibly 5'5" tall. "I knew I was in trouble but I stepped up to him."

"You work here?"

"Yes, I'm the one who founded the Clinic."

"Well, let's talk about this."

With that, the basketball player put his arm around Dr. Curry's shoulders and walked him to his car, saw to it that he got safely inside and on his way home.

On the opening day of the Clinic, Dr. Curry summed up the its purpose in these words:

"Welcome to the St. Anthony Medical Clinic. We are dedicated to the restoration of health, hope and human dignity, and the most important of these is the restoration of human dignity. The majority of our patients are not suffering from a life-threatening physical illness, but the vast majority are suffering from a loss of human dignity, which is the usual price the poor must pay for many of the services they receive in the name of charity. This spiritual loss is usually far more devastating than most physical diseases. We are dedicated to treat patients with compassion, in a professional and non-judgmental manner; to look beyond the superficial exterior of soiled clothes, dirty skin or uncombed hair, and see the inner person, the real self of another human being; to reach out and take the patient's hand and say in actions not words, 'Welcome back into the human race.' We pray each day that the Lord will make us His instrument, to minister to the needs of the sick poor and that He will help us to achieve these goals."

"Anyone can build a clinic," says Dr. Curry, "but if there is no heart—no soul—there is nothing. Father and I talked about it to the staff. It needs a heart and soul to function well."

In its forty-fifth anniversary bulletin, the Foundation stated that the Clinic had provided 200,000 health care visits. That 800,000 men and women had been sheltered for the night. That 16,000 job placements had been made.

THE PARADE

God is mentioned in the Declaration of Independence four times. We should honor Him during the Bicentennial.
—Alfred

A parade, Father decided. An Interfaith Bicentennial Parade would be appropriate for the celebration of 1976. So the project was launched.

Many said, "Oh, it can't work, Father." But they were forgetting this was Father Alfred.

Sister Sheila was asked to take over the organizing, which was a full-time job for one year.

Shortly before the actual parade, representatives of various religious groups who would march in the Parade ate at the Dining Room, sharing a meal "with our guests." There were Christians of all kinds, with Jews, Buddhists and Muslims also present.

On June 27, 1976, 231 units representing all who believed in God under any name marched down Market Street to City Hall. Leading the parade in an open car were Father Alfred and Sister Sheila.

The day was quite hot, unusual for cool, foggy San Francisco summers. But 231 units—the Salinas Liberty Belles, the Milpitas Trojans, the San Leandro Royalaires, the Seattle Señoritas, the Santa Rosa Muchachos, the Oakland Imperials—marched proudly along with Christians of many denominations, Buddhists, Sikhs,

Hare Krishnas, Sufis and more. The celebration ended with a Music Festival at the Civic Auditorium that evening.

But this was San Francisco. That same day the Gay Liberation Alliance had its parade. The Alliance marched somewhat earlier and had a different route but paths would cross at City Hall about an hour or so apart. Several parents of the Oakland Imperials—a Chinese community group with drum major, color guard, drum and bell corps arrived early. After getting their children all set, costumes correctly arranged, marching positions secured, the parents settled down in front of City Hall, got out folding chairs and picnic hampers to eat lunch, enjoy the day and wait for their parade.

Suddenly they were rather puzzled to see guys in sequins, lots of makeup and mesh hose dancing on floats to the sound of very loud disco music. A reporter quickly assured the parents that their parade was coming from the other direction. That this was the Gay Liberation Parade and it would move up Market Street before "their" parade arrived; that the two parades were totally independent of each other.

One mother shrugged and suggested, "If they want to stand up and say they're proud, they should—and when they have more practice, they'll get their marching discipline better organized, I'm sure."

THE MADONNA RESIDENCE
AND SETON HALL

*Alfred is a quiet, unassuming person for his own sake
but a vital, dynamic, forceful person when he is pro-
moting the interest of others.*
— Father Floyd

Alfred was always worried about the women of the
Tenderloin. Where could they sleep; where could they
stay—especially the elderly women, easy prey to mug-
ging, attacks and rape. The first action he took to deal
with this problem was to pay for rooms by the night in
a residential hotel right across the street from St.
Boniface and very convenient. This was the beginning
of the Madonna Residence, as it is now known. He had
a year's lease, but at the end of that period, the hotel
was sold and torn down to make way for a parking lot.

Father needed another piece of property quickly.
Brother Joe found a good-sized residential hotel right
around the corner on McAllister Street. The owner had
died very suddenly, and the widow, a former actress,
wished to sell. Joe negotiated the sale.

Alfred and Joe walked onto the premises to inspect
it more thoroughly. In the back of the building was a
small room, a kind of study lined with books. While
most of the hotel rooms were rented out on a long-

term basis, a few rooms in the back apparently were rented on a very short-term, cash basis. It was, as one says, a hot sheets place. The owner had stashed the money and died so suddenly he had not been able to retrieve it. When Alfred found the cash, he told his brother, "Gather it up. It belongs to the widow. See that she gets it."

Legally, it belonged to the owner of the premises, but Alfred was concerned about the widow and felt strongly it was her money.

And so, for a very short time, Father Alfred owned a hot sheets hotel. "The hotel was in pretty good shape," said brother Frank, "It needed painting, some glass work, but nothing serious. We got that done. Several women in the community formed a guild. The residence got its own management. It was all working.

"The basement was a mess, but the elevator which went up all five flights of the building stopped in the basement, which gave Alfred an idea."

"'I want to fix this up, so the ladies can come down here to sew, to read, to watch TV, to visit.'"

"But when the elevator shaft was built there was no air for the boiler equipment and the heating system, so we had to get an air line built from the roof down the elevator shaft for combustion air for the boiler and the gas heating system. Everything was going great. John Korbus [chief of maintenance] came in to do the whole inside of the basement, sheetrock the walls, put in the flooring. Got it all done. Everything was ready.

"Then a problem developed. The heat would come on, would reach a certain temperature; the thermostat would turn off the heat but with a puff, the pilot light would go out. Oh, no big problem, I thought. I'll light the pilot."

Frank told a helper to let him know when the heat went off. "Call to me down in the basement and tell me you are turning it off. I'll see what happens." When the man gave the signal, Frank "took a roll of tightly wadded paper, lit it, walked over to the boiler, and the whole thing exploded. It burned my hair off my face and my arms, and I was blinded with a flash burn. A woman upstairs called down, 'Mr. Boeddeker! Mr. Boeddeker! Are you alive down there?'

" 'Yes, I guess so.' "

Frank was taken to emergency and treated. When he returned to the hotel, everyone was out of the building, standing on the street. Smoke had gone up the elevator shaft, onto every floor and into all the rooms. So the entire building had to be vacated.

"It scared the hell out of me. I have never again been able to light a match near a gas heater. And my brother Alfred, he acted just like family: 'What's the matter with you? I thought you knew better than that.'"

No sympathy for Frank, who was able to drive home and had no permanent damage. The building *did* get fixed up the way Alfred wanted it and became a very pleasant home for poor, elderly women.

Sad to say, it could not remain that way. The property was in a prime location, near City Hall and several State buildings. The University of California decided to build Hastings Law School in the area and needed the McAllister property. So Alfred went back to brother Joe.

"I need a new building."

Joe quickly found a doctor's hospital at 1055 Pine Street, the old Callison Hospital. It was in excellent condition and the asking price was $1,200,000!

"Forget it. Can you get them down?"

"Maybe a little."

Mrs. Felix McGinnis called. McGinnis, philanthropist and social leader of the City had been a staunch supporter of Father Alfred since the beginning.

"Every year our foundation gives $250,000 to a charity. We know you are having a problem. This year the money will go to the Madonna Residence."

At that point, brother Joe reported he had gotten the price down to $900,000. Still not low enough. Two members of the McGinnis family called.

"Father, we know you need it and you need it now. Our Foundation will lend you $500,000."

"No, the owners want more."

Suddenly an alcohol rehabilitation group wished to buy the property, which did not please the owners of the nearby St. Francis Hotel or the Mark Hopkins Hotel only a block up Nob Hill from the hospital. Father was then able to buy the building at an even lower price. With the money he got from the University of California and by selling two pieces of property adjoining the hospital, he was able to pay back the $500,000 loan to the McGinnis Foundation and have $35,000 left over to remodel the building.

The elderly women were transferred to the new Residence. Each had her own private room. New arrivals were encouraged to bring an article of furniture or a favorite memento from home to represent continuity in their lives. The Madonna was for ambulatory ladies in reasonably good health. The building was safe and comfortable to give them peace of mind and heart. There was 24-hour security, and all rooms had a call bell for emergencies. The Residence had its own cook; groceries were sent from the Dining Room, providing the women with two meals per day. And on each floor there was a small kitchen where they could prepare a cup of coffee or a light snack.

Some residents originally were paying as little as $35 per month. Today, it still has its own guild with a membership of more than 500 people. It also has its own management. Benefits are organized from time to time and bequests help to keep it running. There are always needs. Repairs must be made to the building, furniture needs to be replaced, drapes and curtains must be bought. The list goes on and on. Parties need funding . . . Christmas, Thanksgiving, Easter, Valentine's Day. For each birthday, there is a small party with cake, refreshments and a gift for the birthday lady.

One resident recently commented that, at the age of ninety, she is visually impaired and on a fixed income. The Madonna Residence provides her with a secure, affordable home so she can remain active as a volunteer at two hospitals and assist with benefits for AIDS organizations.

While in residence at the Madonna, artist Eugenia Gogalowska painted two portraits of Father Alfred, which now hang in the Foundation Reception Room. One of them was used as the cover of this book.

For Alfred, money for these ventures seemed to "just come." His brother Frank tells a story of working in the library at St. Anthony's when a woman came up to him and asked, "How do I see Father Alfred?"

"Oh, tell that woman over there. She is his secretary."

"I did but she said Father was very busy."

The lady went upstairs to wait some more; two and a half hours later she was still waiting.

"Are you still here? In a half an hour he will come through here on his way to lunch."

Later Frank asked his brother if the woman had finally seen him.

"Yes, she did. She sat here for three and a half hours waiting for me, and she gave me a check for $10,000. She said that she knew I was working on this Madonna Residence for elderly women and she wanted to give it to me personally. Imagine waiting over three hours for that."

The St. Anthony Residence at 908 Steiner Street was established in 1951 as a home for around forty men. It was the home of the working crew of the Dining Room. Later Seton Hall, as it was known, was moved out to Guerrero Street in the Mission District of San Francisco. Here men who worked in the Dining Room received lodging, clean rooms, showers, personal items such as shaving material plus three meals per day. They were free to leave when they felt ready to re-enter the mainstream. In one twelve-month period, 250–300 such workers passed through Seton Hall with the hope that they could made it back to a productive, happy life.

In 1981 Alfred commented, "If anyone told me all those years ago when we started the St. Anthony Dining Room that we would end up serving over 14 million meals to the poor of San Francisco, I would have thought they were crazy. But looking back—it just happened."

Once pressed about the size and the resources of the Foundation, he answered, "It is big. God is good." One man closely associated with Alfred laughed at this. "Big! That was the understatement of the week. I didn't know how big. Only Alfred knew that. Yes, it was big."

THE INTERNATIONAL CENTER

Be generous, make friends. Don't make enemies.
—Alfred

In 1963 Archbishop McGucken asked Alfred to take over the YLI and YMI (Young Ladies' Institute and Young Men's Institute) building at 50 and 70 Oak Street and run it. Alfred promptly renamed it the International Center, and he had lots of ideas what to do with such a center. It had come to his attention that many foreign students, attending the University of California in nearby Berkeley, and other San Francisco area universities and colleges, were going hungry or had to return home because their funds had run out. In order to help them, he set up a dining room in the old St. Boniface School where around 150 foreign students per day could get a good wholesome meal for around twenty-five cents. This was totally separate from the Dining Room.

Seventy Oak Street became the Foreign Student Center. It was a clearing house for more than 3000 foreign students representing almost all the nations of the world. It allowed them to meet each other and American students. It aided in problems of finance, job hunting, housing, social activities and anything else that was a burden for visiting foreign students. The students had activities, sports, a center to meet where they could relax and study, plus low-cost lunches. Alfred hoped these

116

students who had had tough times would go home with positive feelings about their studies in the United States, about this country and its people in general.

Fifty Oak Street was the local headquarters of the People to People Program founded by President Dwight D. Eisenhower with Father Alfred as the President of the San Francisco International Chapter. It was a voluntary effort of private citizens to advance the course of international friendship. Naturally, Father agreed with these principles to foster understanding among peoples, races and religions. Part of this program was an Envoys Club for consular officials and diplomats, a place to meet, relax, talk to fellow diplomats and also hold meetings.

Alfred represented the National Board of Trustees when he presented the People to People plaque to the Russian Cosmonaut Georgy Beregovoy on his visit to San Francisco (October 27, 1969) "with a warm handshake all around and an embrace of friendship between General Beregovoy and Father."

Also headquartered in the building on Oak Street was the Arab World in America, organized around July 1974. Dr. Teefik Saad was the president. The idea was to help Arabs living in the Bay Area with problems of adjusting to life in this country. Unfortunately, when Dr. Saad died suddenly of a heart attack in 1980, the work stopped.

The large Art Deco ballroom with a capacity of 500 people with the adjoining professional kitchen was often rented out to various organizations for dances, receptions and parties. Memberships were available for people to use the gymnasium, the swimming pool (which had dressing rooms and showers for men and women) two handball courts, a basketball court with gallery for spectators, badminton and volleyball courts and an exercise room.

The buildings also housed the Spring Gardens Senior Center, the St. Boniface Federal Credit Union, Birth-Rite, Women for Peace, the U.S.-China Friendship Association, the Young Ladies' Institute and the Young Men's Institute. Office space was rented to Catholic Social Services, which Father felt coordinated well with other programs in the building, such as services to the aging, work with parishes and religious communities, and the Little Children's Auxiliaries.

For a time, Father also ran Pan-Africa House, a center and meeting place for the benefit of students from Africa.

ADULT BENEVOLENT
ASSOCIATION

I won't give to any church, not any, but I will give to that man.

—A San Franciscan, after
hearing Alfred speak

In 1976 Alfred spoke of the many elderly in San Francisco of whom a goodly number were alone. At that time sixty percent of those eating at the Dining Room were elderly.

"Their needs are not just for food. Oh, the lonesomeness and the muggings and the scary life and oh, my dear . . . so we're trying to come to their aid in every way we can, and that's going to be a big push because these people are the new breed of poor, and to be sick and poor and elderly . . . that's tough.

"There are 137,000 elderly in the City of San Francisco, and 40,000 of them are living alone. The state and the Church as institutions simply can't take on all their problems.

"Inflation has turned old-age security into a nightmare and herded them into dingy hotels or sleazy one-room studio apartments. When the hot plate is turned on, it's a kitchen; when a bed is pulled down, it's a bedroom; when you change your mind, it's a dining room."

More and more elderly were eating at St. Anthony Dining Room, especially toward the end of the month when their meager resources were used up. But it was more than hunger that brought them. It was also loneliness, fear, isolation, illness and despair. Those in the Tenderloin were the worst off.

Father liked to call them mature people instead of seniors or elderly. That had more dignity, and he believed that first and foremost, these people should have dignity. He had already started a group of volunteers in 1969 called Outreach. These were young people as well as elderly who made contact with shut-ins to bring them a little comfort and a few necessities of life. The idea was also to bring them into contact again with the outside world. People in private homes, hotels, hospitals or institutions had often lost that contact. Most had physical or emotional disabilities. Later the group was led by Sister Sheila. She organized volunteers to visit them, talk to them and give them human contact. The volunteers helped the elderly deal with day-to-day problems and also helped in crisis situations. That group became known as Interserv.

But the needs were greater than Outreach or Interserv could deal with, which led to the founding of the Adult Benevolent Association in 1975. It was an umbrella organization whose stated goals were that "We accept and determine to meet on a personal, dignified level, the concerns of older people." These concerns of people on limited incomes, living in tiny apartments or just rooms, frightened by the jungle of crime around them, Alfred determined to meet on a personal, dignified level. He believed that these needs could be met by visits, counseling, supplying food, offering programs to enhance health, education, spiritual and social opportunities. He saw this apostolate as an important commitment, because he saw the elderly as powerless and forgotten.

So why didn't this age group have more political clout? In a city of around 750,000 people, they represented a fairly large electorate, but, as Alfred defined the problem, "Each elderly person complains alone and this plays into the hands of slum landlords. And if they complain or witness against a mugger, a drunk-roller or strong-arm roller, they are then afraid.

"These elderly built the schools and roads, fought the wars, paid for education of judges, prosecutors and law enforcement officials, yet no one speaks for them.

"There is no one with real clout at City Hall helping them. As other neighborhoods are improved, their problems move here: winos, prostitutes, the chronically unemployed and the unemployable. Our officials give the same messages: 'Don't go out after dark,' 'Never go alone,' 'Never answer your doorbell.' In other words: 'You're under house arrest. We can't handle the criminals, so we'll lock you up.'

"So, many of the elderly can't leave their small apartments or single rooms, because when they get back their property may have been stolen. They can't go out in the street for a walk, because they will get mugged. It's a horrible existence—they actually become prisoners, locked up in their rooms in a perpetual state of fear and loneliness. We can't let that continue—something has to be done.

"But taxpayers, who are also people in the pews, are reluctant to take on anything else in the way of social projects. Don't misunderstand me—people are very generous—but many feel that the demands on them are getting too large. Still, something has to be done, and we are going to do our little bit."

One thing he did to call attention to the problem was to hold a summer rally in downtown Union Square.

Several thousand gathered to be entertained and to listen to brief talks on how everyone could help in improving the lives of older persons. That got a good deal of coverage from the local newspapers, radio and television stations. What he wanted was to call wide attention to the problem.

A staff was organized, and dedicated volunteers were found. Concerned people such as students, men and women of various professions, religious persons and other caring people willing to give their time and love were recruited.

Father said the miracles these groups achieved came from people helping people in whatever way it was humanly possible. Those who were wealthy in goods gave help financially; those whose wealth was in time and energy gave of those assets. Such caring Alfred believed was contagious: individual acts becoming the irresistible models for a more caring community. A typical Alfred reaction, "It can be done. Love will make it happen."

Father wanted new projects which would evoke spiritual and attitudinal change and create a renaissance of responsible caring of human for fellow human. He challenged every San Franciscan to join in such a move. "These centers should have an atmosphere of love— counterthrust to the frequent expressions of hate and the muggings and robberies, which are often the lot of these dear people."

He organized all the projects in the Association so that they would interlock and interact with one another on many levels. Some of these projects have already been mentioned, for example, Interserv under the direction of Sister Sheila. This was an interpersonal service particularly important to the elderly in dealing with their day-to-day problems, though it could also provide help in case of a crisis. Requests for service often came from hotel managers of the many downtown residential hotels, district nurses and agencies, as well as from handicapped and lonely men and women of all ages, religions and nationalities—all asking help for themselves or someone they knew. Visits were made to apartments and rooms on an ongoing basis. Sometimes it was to step in to fill a particular and immediate need. Sometimes it was long-range help.

One of the greatest problems was finding housing for the elderly and the handicapped who were caught in the diminishing permanent housing market. As property in San Francisco became more and more valuable, investors moved to buy up old rundown hotels, renovate them into middle-tier tourist hotels or to tear them down and build new, expensive condos or apartments. Sometimes they were just torn down for parking lots. Whole sections of San Francisco had been changed in this manner. Some called it urban renewal, others yuppification. What it meant was there was less affordable housing.

Another aspect of the ABA was the Adult Information Service, a fully staffed telephone information and referral service. One statistic indicated that 30–40 calls came in each week on almost every topic of interest to the aging and their families: legal assistance, housing, health, recreation, employment, transportation. These calls were answered by an informed staff and volunteers.

The Adult Information Center was free to seniors. Approximately 200 people a week would drop in to consult with experts. A Hispanic counseling service was established to help the many Spanish-speaking people living in the area.

The *Adult Information Digest*, a free monthly newspaper for the elderly, contained information on social security, discounts, legal and health issues, event highlights and inspiring editorials—many written by Father Alfred himself. The monthly circulation was approximately 30,000 copies distributed by private mail, through senior centers and churches and to savings and loan offices in the City. This publication served the entire Bay Area.

The innovative Milk Program began in the late 1970s. Its aim was first to supply milk to the elderly, the severely disabled and needy children, and second, to open long-shut doors of fear and loneliness. The program succeeded beyond all dreams and was extended from the Tenderloin to the rest of San Francisco and to Marin and Sonoma Counties. Two nuns of the Congregation of Franciscan Missionaries of Our Lady Queen of Peace from Tijuana, Mexico (stationed in San Francisco) continually toured more than fifty-six hotels and apartment houses, visiting with the elderly they met while helping to distribute milk. Recently more than 130,000 quarts of milk were delivered annually. The giving out of milk was nutritionally sound, but the real reason for the program was to get people to open their doors to volunteers who could talk to them, see how they were doing and help them in any way they might need.

The milk came from the Farm. It was processed for the program by creameries in Sonoma County and resold to the program. Legally it could not come straight from the Farm; it had to be processed first.

Another way to establish contact with the elderly was for the nuns and volunteers to stop people on the street, talk to them and try to assess their needs. This built real bridges of hope and confidence to people who had very little hope or had lost all their confidence. The sisters would follow up by sending greeting cards to the ill and visiting hospitalized new friends. They would often keep in touch when they went on to the Laguna Honda Home—a care facility run by the City of San Francisco—or into other nursing homes. As Extraordinary Ministers of the Eucharist, these sisters were able to bring Holy Communion to shut-ins, giving them spiritual consolation too.

The Mini Market was yet another original program designed to meet the needs of people in the Tenderloin. Once a week, staff members brought fresh produce and meat to the St. Anthony Foundation and sold it to the elderly at a discount. Word-of-mouth advertising made this very popular. For people on small fixed incomes, fresh produce became easily available at a convenient location and at a considerable savings.

For Alfred the interaction of all these projects was fundamental. Interserv found a need, the Milk Program found a new client, that person then could be seen by a volunteer or one of the visiting sisters. Such person's needs and problems were brought to the attention of someone who could help. And sometimes lonely people got out or at least opened their doors to talk to someone once or twice a week. A human contact was again established. A little fear was banished. A tiny bit of light came into someone's life. And the Clinic was available to deal with their health problems.

Father was concerned about the terrible toll AIDS was taking in the Bay Area, and he hoped investigation and research, information and delivery of services could be linked to fight this disease.

In an area such as the Tenderloin, where everyone appears to be dysfunctional and hopeless, Father did not forget the spiritual life. In the midst of this scene, Mass is still said in the different residential hotels. Outings are still arranged to the Franciscan Retreat House in a lovely suburban area across the Bay in Danville. Two buses can take ninety people there even in winter, even in the rain. Tenderloin residents always look forward to the green grass and trees instead of the depressing area in which they live. Rain and cold does not deter them a bit, for the Tenderloin is truly a concrete jungle.

Once someone even asked Sister Sheila for some fresh soil. A woman's plant needed new soil and she asked, "Where can I get dirt in the Tenderloin?" Sister comments that so many are strained for beauty, so many are root-bound. She also points out that this program had been without fanfare or great media attention. The story is that there was no story. Just people in rooms, in tiny apartments, afraid to open their doors, afraid to go out. "We tried to establish contact, to get them to open doors. These people are not interviewed or written about, nor is television interested in them. They are not considered a good story. They are just old people with no contacts—afraid, lonely, often estranged from their families, sometimes with no family."

Spring Gardens at 70 Oak Street was founded in 1977 as an adult center offering spiritual, physical, emotional, educational and recreational programs for adults over 45 years. In 1980 it had a membership of around 450 men and women and a monthly average attendance of 725 people.

The many activities in the social department included trips to Reno or to Sacramento and to other, nearby areas. There were parties for birthdays, Valentine's Day, Halloween, Easter, Thanksgiving and—of course—

Christmas. Tea dances were a popular feature. In addition there were pancake breakfasts, drama groups, bridge clubs, billiards, choral groups, "stone soup" days and brown bag lunches.

The educational department offered lessons in interests such as: needlework, bridge, dance, talent, voice, piano, painting . . . even copper enameling. Speakers lectured on many subjects; favorites included travel slides and films. Good health was promoted with exercise classes, blood pressure checks, health referrals and counseling. Also experts on health subjects were scheduled to speak every month.

On the spiritual side, Mass was said at the Center. There were group studies and discussions of spiritual matters, and the Rosary was said regularly. To help others, Spring Gardens members made gifts for Christmas and donated them to shut-ins, the sick and people in rest homes. Singing groups and drama groups visited nursing homes not only to sing and perform but to make tray favors and provide door prizes. They also mingled and talked to the residents, bringing them a little cheer.

Strybing Arboretum of San Francisco helped Spring Gardens members prepare plants to be delivered to lonely Tenderloin residents. The spirit of giving to others was an important aspect of the spiritual side of the Center.

The Gardens fostered a strong feeling of belonging, of charity and goodwill among members, which spread throughout the community. The members created the programs; they also created an atmosphere of warmth and welcome, which was carefully nourished.

In 1980 three activities were considered outstanding: the Peer Counseling Group, which showed participants techniques of helping others, the Senior Art Exhibit and the Intergenerational Summer Walking tours for seniors led by high school students.

A statement of policy says, "Spring Gardens continues to strive to create an atmosphere which affirms the value of human life, individually and collectively. It recognizes the dignity and worth of the older adult and offers the opportunity for expansion of their creative potential."

Second Spring, a magazine for older adults, was distributed gratis to senior citizens, shut-ins, senior residences, hotels and hospitals. It was noted for its beautiful covers featuring pictures of flowers and trees. It published many interesting and thoughtful articles on different subjects of particular interest to mature people. A private donor gave Alfred a grant for this publication, and Father operated the magazine until the funds ran out.

THE ST. ANTHONY ORGANIZATION

It has to blossom, function or die on its own. The Franciscan Order should never be held liable.
—Alfred

Father Alfred was most concerned that the entire Foundation, Dining Room, Farm, Clinic and the other projects of the Foundation should never be a burden to others, the Franciscans, the Church or the Franciscan Charities. He did it. He put it together. He took total responsibility. He did not want anyone else to be left "holding the bag." He did not want the Church or the Franciscans to be hurt in any way should there be financial difficulties. With good legal advice he set up the Foundation so that it must continue or collapse on its own. It cannot be shut down. Everything must be closed if one part is shut down. So it stands today.

MEXICO

Father was the kind of person who would go up to a person whom he did not know and who might think the exact opposite of what he thought, strike up a friendship and find common ground. That was the type of person he was!
—Father John Vaughn, OFM

In 1941 Father Alfred cofounded the Congregation of Franciscan Missionaries of Our Lady Queen of Peace, with Reverend Mother Catherine de Jesus Rodriguez—sister of a former president of Mexico—and her three companions. The Vicar Apostolic of the northern region of Mexico and Baja California, Monsignor Felipe Torres Hurtado, had recognized the needs of the people of the area and asked Rodriquez to found such an order. Earlier she had tried twice to enter religious life and twice had been told that her health was too fragile for the rigors of cloistered existence. She then devoted herself to the care of her aging mother. When Monsignor Torres prevailed upon her, Catherine agreed but made it clear that she was not free to begin at the time. Only after the death of her mother could she consider such work. When the time came, Father Alfred—with his knowledge of canon law— was contacted in Santa Barbara to help establish the rules for the Order.

The sisters were dedicated to work with the poor of

northern Mexico. Through the generosity of General Ablelaardo L. Rodriguez, a relative, Mother Catherine and her companions quickly acquired property—a large abandoned chicken coop—on the outskirts of Tijuana. Colonia Altamira, as it was called, would become Casa del Niños Pobres and later Casa de los Pobres and the Order's first convent. At that time it was far out of the city. Today with the huge influx of poor from the countryside, the Casa is practically in the heart of downtown Tijuana—which now has a population of more than a million people, making it one of the largest cities on the west coast of North America.

At first the sisters were primarily devoted to the religious education of the young. But it soon became clear that the needs of the poor went well beyond educating their children. What was needed were the basic necessities of life. From the beginning, Mother Catherine committed a substantial percentage of the Order's meager resources—human and material—to provide the poor with food, clothing and medicine.

On a trip to the area in 1945, Alfred noted the dreadful conditions. He asked the people if they wanted a chapel and a free school for grades one to eight. Their answer was, of course, "Yes." An agreement was reached that Alfred would provide the building materials, the supplies and the tools but the people would provide the labor and do the actual building themselves. During construction, Father provided the workers with a hot, nutritious meal each midday. That was the beginning of *their* Dining Room. When the school opened, it was apparent that the majority of students had had no breakfast and brought no lunch with them. So the Dining Room service was continued for them. Then it quickly became clear that their mothers and younger siblings were hungry, so they, too, came to the Dining Room.

Depending upon what was either donated or purchased, breakfast might consist of a combination of milk, refried beans, oatmeal, fruit, peanut butter and—on occasion—eggs. The midday meal would be made up—if possible—of soups, bread, rice, beans, corn, tortillas and meat. Today the Dining Room serves 75,000 free hot meals per year.

With the huge number of people pouring into Tijuana from the countryside, the decision had to be made to broaden the scope of the operation to include all types of help to needy people. They were hungry, lacked sufficient clothing and were in desperate need of medical attention. A privately funded, nonprofit institution was chartered. By 1976 all the necessary legal documentation had been obtained and the operation, on a much larger scale, began. Since there was very little public assistance by the state, the opportunities were unlimited.

All the funding came from donations made by private benefactors, and Father Alfred, through his resources, was the principal benefactor. He traveled to Tijuana three or four times per year even in his late eighties. He lent assistance to the nuns in all of the many fields in which he had experience.

But long before the new charter, much was happening. The feeding of the mothers and children improved the health of the whole family. Students were able to function better in the classroom, and the involvement of the mothers led to whole families being drawn into the project. For example, it was discovered that the extended family was often without food, so a full hot meal was arranged for those who could not come to the Dining Room. Sacks of food were sent home for the housebound. One year 25,000 such sacks were sent home to those unable to come to the Dining Room.

Perhaps the greatest hope in this area of desperate poverty has always been the school. It offers the children an education from grades one through nine, the normal school schedule of Mexico. It has made it possible for students to find jobs out of the barrios and out of the seasonal agricultural labor force. Some children have done quite well and a few have made extraordinary achievements, such as attending colleges and universities. Success such as this serves as an example and a hope for others still in the barrios.

The medical needs, too, were extraordinary, but it was not possible to establish a modern clinic until 1967. Before that, emergency first aid was given by nurses, sometimes with the help of local physicians. After the clinic opened, the number of patient visits gradually increased until 1978 when it stabilized at approximately 16,600 annually. They are treated for a multitude of illnesses, ranging from malnutrition to advanced cases of tuberculosis and leprosy. X-rays, lab work, surgery, orthopedic treatment, dermatology, ophthalmology and dental work are all done at the clinic. Local hospitals see people for special treatment the clinic cannot handle. Some cases are referred to the University of California, San Diego Hospital.

A unique service, in United States eyes, are the prison visits. Five days a week the sisters provide 150 or more prisoners of the Tijuana jail with a nutritious hot lunch. Many prisoners who cannot afford to pay for meals or whose families cannot afford to pay would otherwise receive only a potato and some water each day.

Over the years the Dining Room and its kitchen have been greatly expanded and modernized. Jim Scatena told a remarkable tale related to this. Jim and Alfred had been in Tijuana and San Diego setting up all the necessary warehouses, equipment, refrigeration and transportation to supply food to Tijuana. At the end of a long day, they boarded the plane for San Francisco.

"Well, Father, you have everything set up."

"Just one thing missing, Jim—the food."

"I had totally forgotten about the food!" Jim says. "Every seat on the plane was taken except the one next to Alfred. In the very last minute, a passenger boarded. 'Here comes your food, Father.' I said. It was Henri Levine, the West Coast head of the Hilton Hotel chain. Alfred and Levine had a happy chat, in German, all the way to San Francisco. I didn't understand a word of what was going on, but I had an idea. When we arrived in San Francisco, Father and Levine had made arrangements that the Hilton Hotels would donate any extra food to the Casa, and Levine also promised to enroll the other major hotel chains in the effort. Father had his food."

Jim's only explanation was, "It was a miracle, simply a miracle!"

Henri Levine's story was almost a miracle too. He and his family had fled Germany during the Third Reich, finding Shanghai the only place willing to take them in. There they spent the war years. In 1945 he arrived by freighter in San Francisco and that afternoon had a job as a bus boy at the Fairmont Hotel owned by Ben Swig. Later he became an executive for the Hilton Hotels, managing the West Coast hotels.

Today the Order cofounded by Father Alfred and Mother Catherine with her three companions has grown to nearly 100 members. There are several schools, an orphanage in Nogales for abandoned children and centers for catechism throughout the region of northern Mexico and Baja California. The nuns still comment how they all had a special love for Alfred and that they share his spirit of love and care for others.

In June 1995 the Order served 36,500 hot meals in the Dining Room, including the meals for prisoners; 3250 bags of groceries were given to housebound people. More than a thousand families obtained clothes and house supplies, and perhaps most encouraging of all, eighteen scholarships were awarded for advanced education.

Alfred worked long and hard to help these sisters. At first, he sent them medical supplies. Food came later, obtained especially from the San Diego area. Several problems developed, one of which was that the border authorities would not let any goods enter Mexico without proper authorization and proof that it was not a stolen item. Television sets and electrical equipment, for example, had to have the serial number noted and a confirmation from the previous owners that it had been their property and they were releasing ownership. The nuns could not just come to the border and make the transfer of the goods there. The convent truck had to drive to San Diego, pick up all goods and make certain that all the papers were in order. Later the materials got larger; even building materials and equipment were sent down.

Alfred also arranged for the nuns to come to San Francisco to learn English and computer skills. Once he asked Sister Sheila to find a four-bedroom flat for less than $1000 per month in San Francisco! Unknown to Sheila, the Jesuits of the University of San Francisco found out what Alfred needed and leased him a house for $1 per year.

Another time Sheila tells of Tijuana needing to enlarge a school and wanting furniture. "Alfred sent me out to get it. I dropped everything I was doing. Soon we had tables, chairs, desks, file cabinets. The University of San Francisco was putting in new lab equipment in their science department and gave me all the old equipment. We filled a large Ryder truck and took the equipment down there."

Anita Doyle (better known as La Jolla, California cancer surgeon Dr. Anita Figuerero)—Lady Commander of the Dames of the Holy Sepulcher—has volunteered at the Casa for more than forty years. She organized a support group in San Diego for the Casa (Friends of the Poor) to collect clothing, food and funds for the Casa. Perhaps one of the more touching aspects of their work is distributing Christmas baskets for the children and their families. In addition to food (including a chicken, if possible) there are usually: a toy (such as a stuffed animal or a ball) for each child, an article or two of clothing, and the most treasured gift of all—a blanket to provide a warm cover day and night.

Father's nephew Bob, an electrical contractor in Santa Barbara, for many years drove to Tijuana on weekends to do electrical work and take food and clothes to the Casa. He and his wife adopted a child from the Casa. The mother had died giving birth to the girl, and Bob and his wife, after much legal work, were able to adopt her.

The needs always outstripped the supply. The nuns and Alfred dreamed of doing more for the terminally ill so that they could live, work and die with dignity. Property near Rosario was purchased. It lies on a wind-blown bluff overlooking the Pacific Ocean. This would be the City of Mercy . . . Ciudad de Misericordia. There was a tremendous amount of work to do: roads to be built, electricity installed, a well dug for potable water and a dam constructed to hold irrigation water. Trees and crops must be planted. Only then could construction of the buildings begin. Caretakers were employed to cultivate the land and raise livestock. In the early days, fruit and vegetables—as well as eggs, milk, poultry and meat raised on the property—were taken to Tijuana to supply the Dining Room.

The City of Mercy has a 250-bed hospital for the mentally ill, two 30-bed homes for the elderly, a home for the handicapped and an orphanage for up to 100 mentally retarded children, a treatment center and living quarters for tuberculosis and leprosy patients and a nursery for infants who have been simply abandoned. On the grounds are a cemetery, a large dining room, a chapel, an auditorium and housing for staff and volunteers. The plans were drawn up by Young and Associates of Redondo Beach, California. Pope John Paul II contributed funds. Father worked hard to make the project financially feasible and was the principal benefactor.

When the cornerstone was blessed, Dr. Figuerero stated: "It's an impossible project by human standards. No way can it be done. But it will be done. I don't doubt it."

And the man who put it all together was, of course, Father Alfred, It was his last monumental task.

Alfred also helped by giving expert advice and financial aid to other dining rooms in Mexico City, Leon, Monterrey, as well as to the first one in Tijuana.

ITALY

God is like the sun—always shining, always bright,
but you can turn your back on it and tell yourself it
doesn't exist. Then who is the fool?
—Alfred

Alfred organized the American Friends of the Homeless of Italy to help rebuild war-ravaged houses, villages and towns. He was appalled when, on a trip to Italy in 1954, he saw whole villages still in ruins with people living among the rubble. It had been nearly ten years since the devastation of World War II, but little had been done to help these villagers. He spoke to the Italian community of San Francisco about the situation and his concerns.

Frank Petrini, a prominent businessman and a native of Italy, became the first president of the American Friends of the Homeless of Italy, and many others from San Francisco's large Italian community joined. They chose the village of Maggiore Minori as the beneficiary of a fund-raising drive, culminating in a luncheon held at the Palace Hotel to assess what money had been collected. Jim Scatena was the chairman of the drive and loved to tell the following story.

"We were all so proud to be able to say, 'I have $1,000 or $2,000 or at most, $3,000.' Father was late. He came in the door right at the end of the meeting. I saw him in his Franciscan robe. 'How much do you have, Father?'

I asked. 'Oh, Jim, let me see. $20,000!' It was more than the rest of us had gotten all together. 'Where did you get it?' was the astonished question. 'Oh, it just comes,' he said, but 'I think he has the Archangels Michael and Gabriel in the back room turning it out' was one softly voiced comment in the rear of the room."

In 1979 Father Alfred took, on a few weeks' notice, more than $100,000 to Italy to help the victims of the devastating quake which had hit southern Italy a month or two before. He gave it to the Franciscans of Naples to buy food, clothing, medicine, shelter to cover the immediate needs of the people in the destroyed area.

Another time, with the help of the Friends of the Homeless, he gave technical advice and financial aid to establish dining rooms on the order of St. Anthony's in Naples and Bologna as well as setting up a housing project for the poor in Bologna.

GERMANY

When you have faith in what you are doing and have utter dependence on God, you find the time.
>—Alfred, when asked where he found the time to do all that he did

During the Second World War, Alfred ministered to German prisoners of war in camps in the Santa Barbara area. He gave spiritual consolation to interned men, uncertain of the fate of their families and loved ones. He said Mass, heard confessions and talked to the men in their own language.

After the war, he sponsored the immigration of a number of refugee families to the United States. One person closely associated with this effort stated, "They were in terrible shape." Alfred greeted them upon their arrival, got them apartments, jobs, set them up with furniture and clothes. Most of these families were from Eastern Europe. He also worked with the German-American Welfare Society helping stranded German seamen and other down-and-out Germans in the San Francisco Bay Area with food, shelter and help to get started again or to get back to Germany.

He established a refugee center at Bad Herzfeld in West Germany for people who had fled from East Germany and Eastern Europe. Finally—with funds in the amount of $25,000 donated by Mrs. Felix McGinnis—

Alfred built a church there. Until then the many Catholic refugees in the predominantly Protestant city had had no place for religious services.

For all these services, Father received the Officers' Cross of the Order of Merit of Federal Republic of Germany in July 1954. It is the highest award that republic can bestow. A more popular title for the order is the "Pour le Merite." Begun by King Frederick the Great of Prussia in the late 1700s, it is awarded for particularly meritorious service.

On his first trip to the United States, Konrad Adenauer, the first chancellor of West Germany, had only one request while in San Francisco: to meet Father Alfred. The two men had a long talk. Adenauer complimented Father on his work and urged him to continue what he was doing.

DOMINICAN REPUBLIC

If you give a man a fish, you feed him for a day. If you teach a man to fish, you feed him for a lifetime.
—Often quoted by Father Alfred

On a visit to Higuey in the Dominican Republic in March 1965, Father Alfred was appalled by the wretched conditions of the poor, living in slums at the edge of the city of Santo Domingo. Their misery was terrible, as they were affected by poverty, illiteracy, hunger, unemployment, lack of clothing, and illness. Naturally, serious conditions associated with poverty—such as overcrowding, unsanitary housing and malnutrition—were prevalent. There were no indoor stoves, no indoor toilets or bathing facilities, no running water. In most homes, there was but one common sleeping rack for the entire family—men, women, children and dogs. Father was most concerned with their lack of self-respect and total loss of human dignity.

Alfred, the visionary, the concerned human being and the doer of deeds, organized a group, which raised money for materials. The people were helped to plan and construct their own homes. Even Pope Paul VI was enlisted to contribute money. The funds provided the building materials, the tools and the furniture for homes. The people did the work. Seventy sturdy, prefab, one-level, three-bedroom homes were built. Each also had a kitchen, a stove, an eating area, a living room, closets, windows and doors and perhaps most important, running water, which made possible a bathroom with an indoor toilet.

This project, called Villa Nazareth, solved a specific problem. Possibly of as great importance as the homes, were the feelings of self-respect and pride in the people themselves, because they had been involved in the planning and construction of their own homes. It was not done *for* them but *with* them. It was cooperation not paternalism or colonialism.

THAT TRIP TO EUROPE

If the Lord wants it, He will find a way. Don't worry about the money.
                                            —Alfred

Alfred loved to travel and he dearly loved his family. 1977 marked his fiftieth anniversary as a priest. It was an occasion to be honored. The Archbishop celebrated a Mass at St. Boniface Church, followed by a reception in the church hall. Present were many Franciscans from the entire California province, as well as friends and relatives.

The following day a family reunion was held at St. Anthony Farm for Boeddekers, Gelhauses, Hartmanns, Dombrinks, Billerbecks, Oppenheims and others from this very large extended family. Around 350 people attended.

That fall a family tour of Europe and Israel was planned. Alfred had remained in close contact with family members in Germany and indicated to them that the American family was coming. It was an occasion which certainly called for a party. His sisters, Anne and Josephine, brother Frank and wife Teresa, nephew Paul, some cousins and close friends flew first to Ireland. From there to Cologne, Germany where a cousin met the group and drove them to Alhausen. Father said a Mass of Thanksgiving in the old church, and the group, German and American relatives who had never met each other, with the exception of Alfred, went to a tavern a short distance from the town. A private upstairs room had been reserved. Brother Frank describes the whole thing with a touch of humor.

"Everyone was there, talking away . . . in German . . . a little English here and there. Well, we managed to understand what they were saying. Drinks came. No one was paying. Then food, stacks of sandwiches. More drinks. We were running up a big bill, and I'm shaking in my boots. There must have been 150 people there. We were having a nice visit, but I kept thinking, 'Who's paying? I sure hope I'm not.'

"I went to Father Alfred. 'Say who is going to take care of this?'

"'Oh, don't worry about it.'

"So okay, I forgot about it—for a while. The next thing I know, Alfred disappears for a few minutes but the party goes on. The Germans then go out and bring back some gifts . . . religious articles, a stola, vestment pieces which they had made themselves, plus a small traveling chalice. It was all very nice. We had a very good time. I didn't speak much German and they didn't speak much English, but we got along. Still there was no bill . . . no charge. I never paid. Again I asked my brother, 'Who paid?'

"'None of your business. These things go on like this . . . maybe someone paid for it. It isn't important.'

"The party continued on to the old Gelhaus family farm home, which the Americans found fascinating. Later they visited the town cemetery. Then on to another house belonging to the Pelizaius family—Alfred's grandmother's ancestral home. It had a tile inscription over the doorway which said in German, 'I drive a fast horse but I don't know who feeds it.'"

Frank thought it appropriate for the party.

The group went on to Rome and then to Israel, where Father's dear friend Adrian Falk was visiting and could make good on his long-standing invitation to Alfred, "If you ever come to Israel, I want to show you that country."

Falk, in addition to his donations to Alfred, had been very generous to many Jewish causes. He had given a wing to the University in Israel as well as building a hospital addition. Alfred had been in the Holy Land several times since his student days but now Falk personally drove Father and his party about the country.

Frank observed: "Falk was very religiously minded man. He saw to it that Alfred had all the things he needed and wanted [for the Dining Room]. The two men had great mutual respect and a deep affection for each other. Adrian was always at Father's side. He had Father going to every kind of function there was [in San Francisco] to meet people. Sometimes I thought Adrian was really trying to convert Father to the Jewish faith."

Frank told another interesting story about when the group was at the Mount of Olives. Father was reading the Sermon on the Mount from the New Testament. "Blessed are the poor ... blessed are the hungry ... blessed are the peacemakers ...." It was a deeply moving occasion hearing these words at the place where Christ preached them. All were sitting under a tree. Frank glanced up at it and realized it was totally unfamiliar.

"I never saw a tree like that before. There was a big seed pod hanging down, so I started throwing rocks at it. Finally I knocked it to the ground. There must have been fifteen or so seeds in it. I put the thing in my pocket. Later I took the seeds out and carefully wrapped them and put them in our suitcase.

"When I got home, I gave eight seeds to the brother in charge of the gardens at the Old Mission. He wanted to plant them in the Sacred Garden. I kept the rest in a vase in the dining room cabinet. No one ever touches that cabinet. Months later I got a call from the brother. He couldn't find the seeds I had given him. It was spring and he wanted to plant them. Could he have mine? Sure, no problem. And mine were gone too. We looked and looked, but not one seed ever turned up."

RETIREMENT

*He was in the office six days a week from 6AM to 10PM.
After he was done with a day's work, done with the
church, done with his duties at St. Boniface's, Mass,
devotions, confession and what else came up, he returned to his office. If I wanted to get to him in a personal, private way, I knew he answered his phone himself between 7 and 10PM. Meanwhile he was extraordinarily well read, did a great deal of writing. And he
was awake at 5AM.*
                                    —Frank Schepergerdes

In the winter of 1979-1980, Alfred was in Rome, attending a Franciscan conference. This is when he also
brought the money to help the earthquake victims.
When the conference ended, Alfred traveled to the Far
East to help brother friars in that part of the world set
up programs to help the poor. Alfred was seventy-eight,
in good health but carrying an enormous administrative burden.

His superiors took a good, long look at all his enterprises, noted Father's age and realized that the job was
a killer, even for a much younger man. The California
provincial office decided it was time for Alfred to retire
... for a new administration of the St. Anthony Dining
Room. He was relieved of his positions as pastor of St.
Boniface and as director of the St. Anthony Foundation.

Alfred never voiced his disappointment and gave full cooperation to his lay successor. The family could feel his sense of loss, but Father never voiced any regrets. Again for Alfred, it was obedience to God's will—and time to start something new. This was an opportunity.

At his retirement banquet he made the statement, "You think you have a position and you think that position is important, but everyone can be moved from such a position."

A NEW CHALLENGE

He was the most conventional of men who did the most unconventional things.
　　　　　　　　　—A niece

Alfred was in his late seventies, in good health, with a great deal of energy and a desire to do things he had not been able to do before, simply because he hadn't had the time. Now there would be time.

But, the family suggested, he should get some rest first. A Pacific cruise was just the right thing: no telephones, no interruptions, no schedules, plenty of fresh sea air and solitude. A former mayor of the City made the trip possible, and Alfred embarked on a long cruise. Several members of his family made the cruise with him but said they never saw him. He was in his cabin working furiously on his study of angels—their existence, their influence, their power and their importance. By the end of the "rest cruise" he had a suitcase full of notes for the books he wished to write on the subject. Upon his return to San Francisco International Airport late at night—and not at all unlike many other travelers—he found his luggage (containing all his notes) was missing. He was terribly upset. All his work and effort from the last weeks . . . lost!

"Well, I can't worry about it. I shall just tell the angels to do something about it. I'm going home and get some rest."

The next day Alfred received a phone call. "I seem to have gotten your suitcase."

"Where are you? Who are you?"

"Never mind. I'll send it over in a taxi, and as for my name . . . it isn't important. Just call me Michael!"

Father did complete his work and published it. There would be many other projects Alfred would be involved with in the years ahead. These would be local, national and international. He would now draw on his years of experience as an administrator to set into motion an amazing number of activities.

ALFRED THE PHILANTHROPIST

Anything for that man. My good friend.
— George Christopher

Yes, Alfred was seventy-eight; yes, he was retired. But not quite. A man of his talents and energies could not be idle very long. There were so many things to do. In 1982 he and a group—among them Dr. Curry and Father Phillip Bouret, Society of Jesus, a remarkable Jesuit who had been a missionary in China—founded a nonprofit corporation called La Madre de los Pobres, Mother of the Poor. Its goal was to further health, human dignity and humanity, and it was dedicated to serve the poor, the hungry, the homeless and the sick—especially children. Its board members had a wide range of experience and expertise working with the poor at home and abroad. Alfred was expert in providing for the hungry, Curry was expert on health matters and Bouret on communication.

La Madre's first project was in the Tenderloin. Its immediate goal was to provide shelter and care for impoverished pregnant women who chose to keep their babies instead of opting for an abortion. The organization also worked to integrate blind with sighted children—socially, academically, at play, at prayer and at work. Another great pressing need in the Tenderloin was to help the children of the area, whose daily experience was poor nutrition, inadequate housing, little or no medical care, drug and alcohol abuse and emotional deprivation. Many were latchkey kids surrounded by prostitution, venereal disease, AIDS and drug-dealing. Among the first things La Madre did was organize a Pediatric Clinic for children aged 6–12 providing examinations, diagnosis, treatment, immunizations, disease prevention and counseling programs in drug, alcohol and sex abuse. An Adolescent Clinic for children 13–16 provided similar services, plus education to help them cope with social conditions surrounding them. There were structured recreational programs to divert children from street life and also job training programs to help them become self-supporting, responsible adults.

On the international level, Father had already in 1981 established a modern outpatient treatment program and clinic for the care of lepers in Nicaragua, which led to the abolishment of the Old Leper Colony. No longer were lepers isolated. They were treated, cured and enabled to take their place in society. The following year he established a rural medical clinic for the poor in Darios, Nicaragua, where there were many untreated lepers. Leprosy was easily and successfully treated with modern medications, as were many other diseases rampant in the area.

In the following years La Madre became active around the world, but especially in Latin America and Africa. One of its first large projects in 1984 was a community health center in central Mexico. There followed an immunization and health education program in Guayaquil, Ecuador, and another health program was set up in Guatemala.

Shortly after the start of those programs, Father and Dr. Curry—with the help and cooperation of the World Health Organization, the Pan American Organization and the Medical Mission Society of New York—traveled to Ecuador at the invitation of the local bishop. They arranged for a team of eight health specialists to work in the field for eight weeks. The aim was specifically to train local doctors, nurses and nuns in the newest techniques of public health. A month after the team completed its work, Father Alfred and Dr. Curry went back with four people on another team to educate more of the local medical community.

Even more important than treating people was educating the poor of the area to the benefits of health care. Dr. Curry commented, "The poor see their most important needs to be shelter and food. Food to keep body and soul together and shelter to protect them from the rain and elements. Then they need clothing so they are not ashamed, a job and finally—maybe—medical care. Medical care is not high on their list of priorities. The really poor say to doctors and medical people, 'Everyone is sick, so—that is life.' To get them to understand the need for a doctor is the hard part.

"Leprosy is still rampant in many remote areas. Undiagnosed lepers work in the fields with children who are disease-free. Such lepers work until their hands and feet are just stumps. And the tragedy is that today leprosy can be treated on an outpatient basis. People can live—and live healthy lives—if leprosy is treated with modern medication."

Immunization of children was another high priority for these teams. In these poor, remote areas there was an extraordinarily high rate of mortality among the children under the age of six. The teams, with the help of the local doctors, immunized 50,000–60,000 children against all kinds of childhood illnesses. The idea was to transfer the concept of the St. Anthony Clinic to South

America, to train local medical people and to follow up with a steady stream of supplies for the medical community working in the area.

That same trip Alfred met with Father Luis Pation, OFM in Bogota, Columbia and helped the local people set up dining rooms on the order of St. Anthony's. Father and Dr. Curry continued their trip to Lima, Peru, where they met with Father William Declan, OFM and visited two nearby areas: San Mateo and Pampolana. The first had 10–15 thousand people in desperate need of food, clothing, housing, medical treatment. The second had more than 100 thousand with the same needs, plus the additional problem that there was very little water for drinking or sanitation. Small clinics of two or three rooms were not able to deal with the magnitude of the problem. The small dining rooms there could feed only a hundred or so people, barely touching the need. In Chile he also met with locals to help in alleviating desperate conditions found there. He assisted in setting up an operation to feed one thousand people per day— a beginning.

Father's far-ranging charity also included a leper hospital in Talpa, Philippine Islands, which received clothes, bandages and money from him for many years. He provided funds to help in the construction of small homes in Kerela, India. In 1954, on a trip to Europe, Alfred met the famous Father Pierre, "the Rag-picker Priest of Paris," who worked with the poor in much the same way Father did in San Francisco. The two men became great friends, and Alfred visited Pierre whenever he was in Paris. The men had long talks about common problems, and Alfred helped the French priest with his work from time to time.

The Rosary of the Sacred Heart, developed by Father

Alfred, consisted of 33 red beads—one for each year of Christ's life on earth—and the simple prayer "Lord, Jesus Christ, I trust in Your love." Around 1985 Father was instrumental in organizing the Sacred Heart Society, a spiritual organization devoted primarily to the spread of devotion to the Sacred Heart Rosary. Millions of these rosaries were distributed throughout the world.

This project led Father to think about the Year 2000. "That is the 2000th anniversary of the birth of Christ," Alfred pointed out, deciding this should be honored with a campaign to wipe out hunger in the world. Though Pope John Paul II was very enthusiastic about this project, others saw it as "a pretty tall order." But as Father John Vaughn notes, it was typical of Alfred ... "He never took on little ones. And with his faith, yes, if God wanted to end hunger by the Year 2000, it would be done, and Alfred—wheelchair and all—would help." (After a stroke in 1991, Father spent his last years in a wheelchair.)

As part of his campaign to help end world hunger, Alfred became interested in Africa. Food and medical supplies were shipped to Zaire and Zambia. In the Sudan, refugee camps were constructed with the funding from Chevron Oil Company. Unfortunately the continuing, brutal civil war there wiped out the structures.

Eriteria on the Red Sea, near the Horn of Africa—recently independent from Ethiopia after a long, harsh war—came to Father's attention. The war left Eriteria one of the poorest countries in the world—just as poor and just as hungry as nearby Somalia, which had received worldwide attention. At a Mass at Santa Clara University, several Eritreans came to a member of La Madre organization and said, "Send food to Eriteria. The people are starving."

To the question of what was most needed to help the

people to get on their feet to help themselves, the answer was: goats, chickens, donkeys. Goats for milk; chickens for eggs and fertilizer and eventually, meat; donkeys for transportation. A shipment of books went there too—in English, the major language, heritage of a long British presence. Alfred wished to start dining rooms there also. He hoped the Dining Room concept would spread throughout Africa to alleviate some of the hunger on that continent.

With the Fall of the Berlin Wall, the whole of Eastern Europe opened up again to the West. Father Alfred immediately became involved and found a great spiritual need. Priests had been in jail for years and were suffering the aftereffects of their imprisonment. They had been cut off from the mainstream of Catholic thought so long that they now needed theological instruction and seminary preparation. The Church had few ways to reach its people; it needed a means of communication. La Madre de los Pobres was able to obtain radio equipment and ship it to Eastern European countries: the Czech Republic, Poland, the Ukraine and Hungary. With this equipment the local churches could set up Catholic broadcasts and give instruction to people who had long practiced their religion in a semi-underground. Through these radio broadcasts the Church could send spiritual messages to people who otherwise had no contact with priests. Father Methodius of Prague, superior of the Dominicans; Dick Harnett of INS, since retired and living in Daly City; and Father Bouret were all part of and invaluable in the La Madre de los Pobres effort in Eastern Europe.

Food, too, was sent to help feed the needy. People in Hungary asked for food supplies because many ethnic Hungarians in the Ukraine were starving and desperately needed food. The La Madre Foundation shipped food and medications for reshipment to the Ukraine. In Bosnia, torn by a long and bitter civil war, help easily reached people because many of the priests in that Balkan country were Franciscans who had contact with Alfred. One major project was to give goats to rural families. These animals provided them with milk, and if there was a surplus, it could be made into butter or cheese. When goat kids were born, they were to be given to the next family on the list. These goats were not to be slaughtered for food. Only if they were killed by a land mine, could they then be eaten.

When Pope John Paul II visited Ecuador, he said the Rosary in a local cathedral. La Madre arranged for satellite television transmission so that the event was simultaneously broadcast around the world and became known as the Global Rosary.

In the midst of all this, the work in Mexico was not forgotten. Father continued to support the convents in Mexico and work with the nuns there on all their endeavors, especially the City of Mercy.

ALFRED THE CEO

When Alfred stepped away from the altar, he was all businessman. His was a remarkable ability to combine business acumen and spirituality.
—Greta Schepergerdes

It was astonishing that Alfred could do all that he did. He got up at 5AM, said Mass, read, did some writing, talked to brother friars, had breakfast. Even when he retired, he was in his office at 10AM. He kept up this pace almost to the moment of his death.

But rising early and working late did not explain how he could do all he did. And brilliant as he was, the ability to manage his many enterprises did not come instantly and sometimes not easily. Alfred learned but he often learned the hard way by making mistakes. He learned from them and he profited from them. There is an old saying, "If you don't make mistakes, you are not doing anything. If you make too many, you get fired."

In the early days, the Dining Room grew at an astonishing rate. The major problem was to keep it operating. The organization was minimal and not always consistent. Father realized he needed expert help. He asked for and got it from many people. Two men among many others who gave Father invaluable lessons in business methods were his brother Joe, long an executive with

159

Southern Pacific Railroad, and Adrian Falk, the well-known philanthropist.

From Joe Father learned businesslike organization. Joe was a detail man . . . every single detail. He showed Father how to set up plans with the use of binders, each binder with all the details of a project, all carefully organized. Beth Payne commented, "Father learned so much from Joe."

Falk, who came into the picture around 1954, wanted to help Alfred get off the ground. "I came from the bottom up; I know." He gave Father a basic education in business and management.

From canon lawyer and theologian to business CEO of a large corporation took time to learn. It was not easy. But logical clear thinking, identifying problems and dealing with them systematically and logically is good business practice. It is also good law and good theology.

Frank Schepergerdes remembers the business lessons Alfred had in the car. "I drove. Father and Adrian were in the back seat talking. The advice was real."

"You have to go to the people who run this city to get big help," Falk had advised, "Make the people who run the city help you.

"Father, if you really want something . . . think big, operate big, and when you really want something, you have to go to the top, not below that. The people below have to go to the top, so you cut out all the influence along the way. There might be someone along the way who doesn't like you or who doesn't like your cause. So your proposal might never get to the top. Go to the top and then work down. If it comes from the top, the bottom will help. They're all scared for their jobs."

Alfred networked long before the term was popular. He was constantly expanding his contacts. It wasn't important that people gave. It was important to meet them, to know them, to show them the need. If they were not ready to give, Alfred sensed it very quickly and changed the subject, talked baseball, maybe. Frank Schepergerdes, who went with Alfred to the big homes in San Francisco and the Peninsula, remarked:

"He had his unique style. He wanted introductions. He would remember people's names, places, faces, and he would effectively use them as information. 'I met so-and-so.' He was great at networking . . . great, in that he believed in expanding his contacts. 'The more people you get to know, the better it is. It doesn't matter if I get anything, as long as I have met them. If you can know the people and show them there is need, they may not be ready for it but it will come. Maybe in a month, six months, a year. Maybe never, but that is fine too. It will come. They will see the need.'" Meanwhile Alfred met people and established contacts, because, "The more people you know and the more you get known, the better it is. I simply say, 'This is what the problem is . . . .' Let them take it from there. I don't have to ask. If they want to help, they will."

"Alfred had a unique style with people," Frank continued, "simple, straightforward. And he was getting money for the Lord.

"Alfred was a dreamer. We would be riding in the car, and he would throw out things . . . ideas. They made no sense to me at all. They might not make any sense but he wanted me to hear them and think about them. Sometimes nothing would be said about the ideas for a long time. Then when it really got down to it, when he really wanted to do something: 'Frank, get out a pencil and paper. We are going to start this thing from the bottom up.'

"Alfred would be very factual. There wasn't a thing he would miss to prepare for a new venture, to prepare for a new building, to prepare for the unknown. Research was done. He got me to do a lot of that. By the time weeks had gone by, there was a very clear picture of what was going to happen. There were steps: one, two, three, four, five. 'What is the cost . . . leave room for the unforeseen.' He was very methodical, so the project would not—maybe could not—fail. People thought he didn't care about details. Don't kid yourself. I would drive the car. He would have his pad in hand and make notes. We would talk back and forth."

Alfred kept a little booklet. "Oh, by the way" and he would run something by people he trusted . . . people he knew were not yes men. His brother Joe, his younger brother Frank and his farm manager and cousin by marriage, Frank. These were people who would say, "It isn't working." These people he knew would tell him exactly what they thought and not just try to please him. These were the men he used as his sounding boards. Brother Joe at Sunday dinner at Joe's home or at his daughter's house. His brother Frank from Santa Barbara, who came up frequently to work and, after retirement, spent an average of ten days a month in San Francisco working for Alfred—especially electrical work on the various buildings—all gratis. Frank Schepergerdes at the Farm where Father would go on his day off.

Alfred trusted his brothers and Frank. It was very important to him that his ideas, his plans and whatever he said would not go any further and would not come back to haunt him. And he needed opinions.

Alfred was not mistake-proof. He had his problems with employees and with locals who betrayed his trust and stole from the Dining Room. One was a supposedly reliable Dining Room employee who took butter and other things from the Dining Room around the corner to a local cafe, where he traded them for his hearty breakfast of ham and eggs every morning. Office equipment such as typewriters and other supplies were constantly disappearing in the early days. The police would bring in merchandise which had been hocked or found in a raid, "Is this yours, Father?" Sure enough. He learned through these incidents to put tighter controls on the Dining Room and office premises to keep down the thefts.

Another example was a very trusted employee who would say, "Father, we need this."

"But we bought several two weeks ago. Where are the ones we had?"

"I don't know, Father. Someone must have taken them."

"Well, go get some more. We need them. We can't work without them." Finally Alfred's brother Frank—while working on a job with that employee—noticed all the missing tools and machinery stashed away at a site. The someone who had taken them was the trusted employee, and he had set himself up very nicely in his own construction business, courtesy of Alfred and the Dining Room. He was promptly let go. Typically, he later spread stories that Alfred was lazy and incompetent.

In later years, the Dining Room was buying federally subsidized food, such as butter, beans and canned meats. The boxes were clearly marked "Not for sale or to be given away." Alfred was scrupulous in following these guidelines. The boxes were emptied, then recycled and used to ship supplies to Mexico. Apparently someone with a grudge reported the shipment of the boxes to Mexico, making the assumption that they contained the federally subsidized foods. A long federal investigation followed. Alfred and the Dining Room were cleared. There had been no violation of the regulations. But it was embarrassing to Alfred to be placed under such a cloud of suspicion.

Then there were times when Alfred's heart may have taken priority over his head, as Frank Schepergerdes relates.

"One day he came to me—I couldn't believe it—and says, 'I'm about to go and sign the papers this afternoon to take over St. Joseph's Hospital for an old people's home.'

"I'll never forget it. I threw my hands up and said, 'You have got to be kidding. You have just got to be kidding.'

"'Why?' from Alfred, who did not like to have his judgment questioned that strongly.

"'That's all you need now—to put that big a thing on your back. Where is your control? How do you control that? I don't think you want this thing to flop. Everything else has been a success. Have you done enough homework to really get this thing under your belt?'

"He got furious. His face was white. I knew him. When he was mad . . . he was mad, real mad. He had a good German temper. I wouldn't let him get away with that. I always felt I owed him an honest answer. He could do with it what he wanted. He didn't have to do what I said. But he came to me and wanted an honest reaction, and he got that.

"Alfred didn't sign the papers that day; he stalled on the purchase. He thought over what I said. It was too big an operation. Who would run it? I said, 'From my point of view . . . from where I'm sitting, it doesn't sound right. It doesn't feel right.' That is what he came to me for, and that is what he got. He never did take over that hospital.

"He had the Dining Room, the Farm and all the other things. He was pastor of St. Boniface, extremely well read, he wrote, worked until 10PM. The man didn't sleep. He had a great way of doing financial things— costs, how to go about something, hauling, all the things that go into a business. As an example, he called me at the Farm. He needed to replace the shower stalls for the swimming pool at the International Center. The contractor was to tear out the old showers and replace them with plastic stalls—for $12,000.

"'How many shower stalls are there?'

"'Eight.'

"'That's $1500 per shower for plastic? Have you had this looked at by someone else? You are being had, I would say. We put in a shower here at the Farm with real tile for $800.'

"'Frank, call someone. Get another price.'

"So I called a man in Santa Rosa and told him the story. Eight showers—figure the worst possible mess to clean up—figure how much . . . roughly. The answer, 'Eight showers . . . say 900 bucks in tile.'

"I called Alfred back with the Santa Rosa estimate. This is how he was successful. He went to people who could help him and asked questions. He not only asked the questions but listened to the answer. Then he made his own decision. And he admitted it when he was not certain.

"He had a way. He made people feel he knew nothing about a certain situation. He needed their advice and help. 'Could you help me . . . tell me what to do in this situation.' Most people want to help, especially for a good cause. That was his method to involve people: 'I'm only a Franciscan.' That guy was so foxy. He knew how to make it work. You couldn't help but admire him, because of what he did with it. He used it all for the poor. He got a bang for the buck. People knew that 90–95 cents of every dollar contributed got to the poor. There was almost no payroll, around eight people on a salary and all the rest were volunteers. If he wasn't doing it for the poor, you would have run him off.

"He had a philosophy, 'Don't tell people ahead of time what you are going to do. Tell them when you are doing it.' He was so low key. He never asked. He never said, 'I'm going to do this or that.' When the Farm was just getting off the ground, I often asked, 'Why don't you publicize it more, Father?'

"'Just wait. When the time comes. When we have something to show people. Then we can show them.' When the time came, people came: church officials, media people. But Father never said. 'Look what we did here.' He just took them around, showed them everything and had the men answer questions. 'The Farm can speak for itself. Let them see what we did. We don't have to tell them.'"

And he was a good administrator since, as one man noted, he was good at getting someone else to give out the bad news.

People were often astonished at his personnel management. When his longtime accountant died, he told the young assistant to make a list of requirements for the position. She did and took it to Alfred.

"When do we start interviewing?"

"We already have someone."

"Who is it?"

"I'm looking at her."

"What are you saying, Father?"

"I'm saying you're it."

Laurie had come to the Foundation as a 19-year-old

just out of high school. She had ability, which Alfred recognized and honored.

Sister Sheila remembered, "You got a really nice feeling from him. You don't always get that from other bosses, that you are recognized and appreciated. He would take us out to lunch at a nice restaurant. The Spinnaker in Sausalito was a favorite; Castagnola's on Fisherman's Wharf was another. I found out much later he was not paying for anything. He knew the owners and they never gave him a bill."

Someone else commented that Father's frequent personal visits to—and his support of—his employees on the job was the secret of his success in keeping their loyalty and hard-working attitude. He was never too busy to listen and to understand their needs and problems.

Alfred gave people the space to do as much as they could do and become as much as they could become. He gave the gift of hope. One person, a recovering alcoholic, commented, "We came to the Dining Room in a bad place. Alfred made us realize we were of use to others. Wherever we were, there was someone in more trouble than us who needed our help. If we failed, they were in worse shape, so we had to do the best we could ... whatever that was. Maybe as a start sweeping the floor. Artists, writers, a former Wall Street stock broker, executives and just plain people found their way back this way. By working, you were producing and, in time, you could do more. It was wonderful."

One reason Alfred had such wide support was that people knew the contributions went to the work—not to administration. In a 1977 interview Father said, "Look at this desk. This, all the furniture you see in this room is secondhand. We have no overhead, no bureaucracy, no salaries."

Years later employees were paid adequate salaries, and a pension system was put in place. Many had worked long years at very low salaries, and this was a boon in their old age.

Beth Payne commented, "Father was very strict about money handling. Money might be given to him with the comment 'This is to buy vegetables for the Dining Room.' And that's where the money went. Always, always, always. Or, 'This is for Mexico' and that's where it went.

"Then there were unattached funds. 'Do anything you like with this, Father.'"

One donation with a specific request resulted in a funny incident. A young refugee from Germany was the bookkeeper. She banked some money Alfred gave her, and at the end of the week, it turned up in the wrong account.

"What's this doing in the Farm account?" Father asked. "It should be in the foreign students' account."

"I saw your notation—'for stud'—and thought it meant for a stud; i.e. a bull. So it had to be the Farm."

"No, no, for foreign students."

Beth commented further, "He was always doing. It was incredible how much he did. His mind was always going. 'Keep Busy' was his motto."

A reporter after an interview with Father said, "If you took away all of Alfred's work and gave him nothing to do, he would devise a new program in a few hours." The reporter added if he were President of the United States, he would appoint Alfred Secretary of Health, Education and Welfare.

Johnny Jacobsen, a cousin who worked for Alfred on a number of projects, said, "He is the only man I ever met who has the idea, can do the planning, develop it, implement it and then can continue the operation."

Pat McShane, a niece, remarked that Father was one of the best utilizers of mail she had ever seen. He always thanked people for what they did for him and his organizations. One friend of Alfred's came every Saturday for years and wrote out Father's thank you letters, which he would sign later.

So where did all the money come from?

In an age of televangelists who take in $100 million a year, the money Father Alfred gathered seems rather insignificant. The difference may lie in what he did with the money. He seemed to get the maximum usage from all the money he took in. And everything that Alfred took in went where it was supposed to go. It was this trust in the man that enabled Alfred to attract large sums of money.

In the very early days, there was no money. The Dining Room and all who worked there were very, very poor. In the 1970s bequests started to come in. These were the basis of the Foundation, which was organized in such a manner that when Alfred was no longer alive, the work had to continue.

There were very wealthy benefactors who gave to Father Alfred and to him alone, key people who helped put him on his feet from the very beginning. Mrs. Felix McGinnis, Adrian Falk, Cyril Magnin of the mercantile family, Ben Swig—the hotel owner and prominent San Francisco philanthropist—were all supporters.

"Father went to Ben Swig when all else had failed," one man revealed. Herb Caen of the *San Francisco Chronicle* was an early and very loyal supporter who gave the Dining Room a great deal of publicity. Louise Davies, who attended school with Alfred's sister

Josephine and for whom the San Francisco Symphony Hall was named, was a major supporter.

There were golf tournaments and fund-raisers. Once actor Danny Thomas was the guest star at a dinner dance at the Fairmont Hotel. The St. Anthony Auxiliary once published a cookbook . . . no, not recipes of how to cook for 1500 guests in one afternoon, but the favorite recipes of organization members. In the late '70s, Alfred mobilized a giant flea market for San Francisco charities, all kinds of nonprofit organizations, in Brooks Hall. It was a great success and raised money for the Dining Room as well as the other local charities.

But generally, the money came from donors large and small, people who knew what Alfred was doing and gave their dollar, five dollars or ten dollars. Which gave Alfred the resources to do so many different things, including his international works.

Alfred, of course, put it best. "All this just grew. Our money, our food, our help are gifts from the heart."

ALFRED THE MAN

He was a giant of a man—physically, spiritually, morally, with a pixie smile, a great sense of humor and a simple, loving heart.
—A cousin

Dear Abby once said the best index to a person's character is how he treats people who can't do him any good and how he treats people who can't fight back. It was the poorest of the poor and the weakest of the weak for whom Alfred had a special smile and firm handshake.

Frank Schepergerdes said of him forty years later, "He didn't want flashy stuff; he kept it very simple. I cleaned his room; there was nothing in there. Others had stuff—not much—not fancy, but more than Alfred . . . much more than Alfred. He had the barest minimum."

If someone wanted to give Alfred a new car, he wouldn't accept it. He didn't want to have a new car. "Give that to the Church, and let me have that one over there—that used one."

Yet for all his simplicity, Alfred embraced life. He could hear a singer and be enthralled with the voice and the song. He enjoyed a good joke and a story. He loved a family dinner party with the china, silver, crystal and a menu straight from *Gourmet*. He also loved a simple family meal where the hostess wasn't expecting a guest. The country gave him great peace. There he enjoyed the sky, the clouds, the grass, the flowers, the trees and the peace. Travel, people, everything—life itself seemed to give him great joy. Once he said that he defied anyone to try and make him unhappy.

He was an excellent linguist and enjoyed using his many languages. Brother Frank told of going out to dinner with Alfred. "We would ask, 'Do you have a waiter who speaks Italian, German, French, Chinese or Spanish?' Usually there was one person on the staff who could speak at least one of those. He or she would come wait on our table and Alfred would converse with them, ask where they came from, how long they had been in the States, talk about their families, and everyone would enjoy the whole thing."

One of his brother friars commented, "Alfred's confessional had a sign: 'Confessions heard in English, French, Spanish, Italian, German and Chinese.' People must have thought there was a priest in there with two heads."

A person who worked with him for nearly forty years remarked that he never gossiped about people or was derogatory about anyone or his work. There were one or two exceptions to this, where after long abuse or lack of work the person had to go, to Father's regret.

In the afternoons, he would relax in his reclining chair, pull the curtains in his office, settle back and watch some soaps. *All My Children* was one of his favorites. One evening, prominent friends sent their Rolls Royce to pick up Alfred for a function and then went on to the St. Francis Hotel to pick up actress Ruth Warick. Father kept looking at her, perplexed that he knew her . . . but from where? "Do I know you?" he asked. "Have we met?"

"I've been in movies, and I'm in a TV series . . . ."

"You're Phoebe in All My Children." They became fast friends. She visited when in town and became a great supporter.

He also watched the news, local and national, with great interest. He loved changing channels. He enjoyed The Beverly Hillbillies, I Love Lucy, Candid Camera and especially, on Saturday evenings, The Lawrence Welk Show.

On his day off he would go to the Farm, sometimes to relax, but mostly to talk business with Frank Schepergerdes. Sundays he liked to spend with family—his brother Joe's family, his sister Josephine, nieces and nephews—and then return to the Friary to spend the rest of the evening with his brother friars, his Franciscan family.

Alfred loved to travel and did so frequently: to Italy on Franciscan or Church business, to Mexico quite often to visit Casa de los Pobres, and to Marian Congresses all over the world. This helped to bring him to places needing help—such as Santo Domingo, Central and South America, Germany and Italy. He visited Australia for a Marian Congress and returned on a Pacific Far East liner where he totally relaxed on the long sea voyage. The fresh sea air was a tonic, and the quiet with no telephones and no meetings gave him a chance to be away from the stress of his normal responsibilities. He seemed able to relax fairly easily. He could work to the point of exhaustion, then relax and recharge, be ready to work again at a pace that might kill a younger person.

He would simply go away for a time when he was tired. Only a very few people would know where he was. They had a telephone number in case of emergency. For years it was his brother Joe's house in Oakland. The guest room with the high-backed Victorian oak bed was simply "Father's Room." He kept many of his things there: his reading materials, his writings, letters from close friends and family. He might spend three or four days there, say Mass for Joe and his wife Marie early in the morning, have a small breakfast and then simply disappear into "Father's Room" until evening. He could read, write, sleep . . . totally undisturbed.

In later years he went to Santa Barbara and stayed with brother Frank and Teresa. Frank commented that when Alfred said Mass, he would preach a little sermon to them and discuss theology.

"It got so deep, we had no idea what he was talking about. We had trouble following him. When we asked for an explanation, it got deeper."

Sometimes Alfred would check himself into St. Joseph's or St. Mary's Hospital. The nuns would see to it that he had absolute peace and quiet and would not let anyone disturb him. There, too, he could have a complete rest.

Alfred had terrible headaches most of his life. These seemed to be centered in the back of his head, and rubbing his neck and head was a characteristic gesture. He consulted several physicians, but doctors could not find the cause or give any relief. The headaches did not keep him from his desk or his work.

In later life he was plagued with a hereditary skin problem, a lack of pigment. In the end, his hands were almost white with only spots of normal color. His face and chin had white spots that, with advancing age, got worse. His sisters, Terry and Josephine, had the same problem.

Alfred loved his extended family and managed to research all the relatives on his mother's side who had come to America beginning around 1880. He drew up a chart with names, branches of the family, addresses. It was quite an undertaking since by 1977 there were more than 800 people in the United States belonging to the clan. He sponsored several reunions at the Farm with nearly 300 people attending. He helped his family, finding jobs for some and employing others. There were whispers of nepotism. But as one priest said, if he helped everyone else, why shouldn't he help his own family? And his family was supportive of him. Some were very successful financially and gave a great deal of their money, time and effort to Alfred's many enterprises.

Alfred dearly loved children and could relate to them very easily. Celeste Richard, a great-niece, played with him as with a companion. Her grandmother thought it was disrespectful to be so familiar with a priest, but Alfred did not see it so.

Tony Hartmann was four when he found himself on Father's lap. No hesitation to talk to this man. They discussed helping Mother and found they had similar problems with housework. They had the same nickname and yes, the same given name: Anton . . . the European spelling, not Anthony. They were named for the same man, Tony's great-great-grandfather Anton Hartmann. Both were born in August, Tony on the fifth and Father on the seventh. The eighty-five years between them were not important.

Alfred loved to read aloud to children, especially the books of children's writer Putsy Kelly.

Another time Celeste got a joke book as a gift. "May I see that?" Father asked. "I think I could use it." Poor Celeste never saw her book again. But she saw its loss for a good cause.

When Alfred spoke to anyone, he paid the highest

compliment: his total attention. And whomever he spoke to—whether down-and-outers, prime ministers or presidents—they were all equals to him.

Father Floyd says, "He was a great storyteller. Humor was part of his life, part of his personality. He had a fine mind and was great at organizing. A warm, caring person of great charm. And he had a temper. He could also delegate dirty jobs. There were some very hard times in the Dining Room and all the related projects. Others would have given up. Not Alfred; he hung in there. Perseverance and patience. It took a great deal of patience to deal with some of the people he had to deal with. It was hard for him to see the world changing . . . more violent with more people in need . . . then his faith would jump in."

Alfred was always fascinated by science, astronomy, physiology. He borrowed a niece's nursing books to study. His friend Dr. Scheer taught Alfred a good deal about DNA, which not only interested him, but he saw it as an example of God's handiwork. The concept of the helix gave him the idea for *Spiral*, a spiritual newsletter, which he wrote. "In the Spiral/Helix we shall work together, help one another to reach the heavenly reward."

Alfred said never make an enemy if you don't have to. He tried to avoid a flat-out rejection. "Never tell people it is a poor idea and it won't work. Save people's self-respect if you can. Make some remark, like give it time or why don't we wait and see. I say, 'Let me think about it. I have to give it some thought before I can do something like that.'"

Alfred was a good student. He listened to what people told him and weighed the wisdom of what was said.

"Learn from your mistakes," he advised. "Do not get

buried by them, but learn. Never put anyone on the spot. Never put anyone in a corner. Lead them to it. 'What do you think. How should I do this?'"

Frank Schepergerdes elaborates on this: "When Alfred felt the person didn't want to give information or help, he would simply change the subject. That would be the end of the conversation on that subject. He would never make a person feel uncomfortable. He picked up body language and reactions immediately. 'This was not the time. Maybe in a year.' He did not lose the person in the process. He was able to sense that someone might be worried about seeing him in the future, worried Alfred would remind him of what he had said before. Alfred would never bring the subject up again. The key to his success was not punishing people for their hesitation. 'Never make a person feel guilty. Never bring it up again. If they bring it up, that is fine.'"

ALFRED THE PRIEST

What can one person do in the face of hunger, homelessness and joblessness? Alfred did quite a bit!
—An admirer

Alfred was a priest, a Franciscan Friar, a follower of St. Francis of Assisi, a deeply spiritual man. Alfred believed deeply that God is love and the presence of God is all love. He was enwrapped in the love of God, the power of knowing "God loves me." He believed no matter what a person had done in the past . . . "now trust God, make your peace with God, and it will be all right." Alfred was taken up with the spirit of St. Francis and was conscious of God's presence among the poor. "If I'm going to find Christ in a special way, that's where I'm going to find Christ—among the poor."

Alfred always reached out and touched people on the sidewalk. For years he would walk down the line and shake the hands of everyone there, pat them on the shoulder or give a word of encouragement. He would reach out to them as if they were important, as important to him as anyone he knew at City Hall or in the corporation board rooms. He never saw the guests of St. Anthony Dining Room as a faceless group but always as individuals. Even in a wheelchair, he would roll by and smile, say hello, touch the people and say something positive. That was the spirit of St. Francis. And of Alfred.

He was very active in ecumenicalism, long before it became fashionable. He had good friends in the Jewish, Protestant and Eastern Orthodox communities and worked closely with them. The Greek Orthodox bishop of San Francisco was a good friend. Alfred worked throughout his many years for better and closer relations with the Eastern churches. He was very much interested in all the Eastern Orthodox faiths and worked for the reunification of the Eastern and Western churches.

His brother Franciscan friars were his family. If he went out on Sunday, he made a great effort to get back for supper "with the boys." He did not want the friars to feel left out of his life; so he would get back to play cards and chat. It was a community: his brothers, his support group, his second family. One friar remembered that discussions were often about theology, some taking very different positions from Alfred. He would argue his view very strenuously, and sometimes the other man might feel somewhat "put down." When that happened, Father would be dejected and try to make amends.

In the 1970s when San Francisco, especially, was the heart of student and youthful unrest, Alfred observed, "They appear to be striving for better things. They are discontented. There are certain definitions they are trying to find . . . certain gaps to close. I doubt if today's struggles are too different from those past. It just could be that this generation is coming more to grips with its troubles."

The open homosexual scene of San Francisco bothered him—yet on his book shelf were six or more books on the subject. He wanted to understand.

Disturbed and saddened by a new movement where many nuns and priests were leaving their orders and the priesthood, Alfred had difficulty understanding and accepting these choices. Yet he employed many former nuns and priests in the Dining Room, giving them jobs to help them make the difficult transition back to secular life. Many of them did not have families who would or could give financial or moral support in very trying times. Alfred was there for them.

One group of nuns lost their convent in New York when the old building simply crumbled away under them. They were homeless. When he heard about their predicament, he employed them in the Dining Room until they could find a new convent in which to live— and which he helped to secure for them.

Alfred's first priority was as pastor of St. Boniface Church. In that capacity he said Mass, heard confessions, baptized babies, married couples and buried the dead. He gave spiritual consolation to any and all, regardless of creed, sometimes unexpectedly.

One day a man stood on the roof of the YMCA building—thirteen floors above the sidewalk—threatening to jump. Police came; firemen came. They got within six feet of the would-be suicide when he renewed his threat. Would he talk to a priest? Yes, he would, and Father Alfred just across the street was sent for. Alfred edged close to him.

"George, I'm a friend. I want to see what I can do for you."

"You can't bring back my friend. He's dead."

"Come on in, George, let's go inside," Alfred kept saying, "Come on in, George, let's go inside."

Father later told the rest of the story:

"I got close enough so I could put my hand over his. His was ice cold. Then I slowly tightened my grip until I had a firm hold. I urged him again to come inside so we could talk. Without saying any more, he let me help him over the parapet. The police grabbed him. I told them I wanted to talk to him alone a few minutes. We had a talk. He was grieving for a friend. He had had family troubles since he was a baby. I told him maybe he could come to the Farm."

To people who were troubled—drinking, in a depression or in some other kind of low—he recommended: "Work, work, work. Just work till you forget your trouble." And "Trust. Just trust in God and His goodness."

In the spirit of St. Francis, Alfred blessed not only people, but also animals, plants, projects and other things. Long before Northern California wines became fashionable, Alfred blessed the grape harvests of growers such as Mondavi of Napa County and the Sebastiani family of Sonoma.

AWARDS

If Alfred dressed up in all his degrees, he would out-shine an archbishop any day.
—A bishop friend

It was very natural that many awards would come to Father Alfred. His endeavors were so wide-ranging, his projects so many and varying. Telegrams from presidents were almost routine. There were resolutions from the State of California legislature and citations from various governors. The City of San Francisco honored him many times. In addition there were the local and regional awards. He received the Laura Bride Powers Award for his contribution to the City and the Pro-Life Award from the United for Life Organization. In 1976 St. Ignatius College gave him the President's Award as the "Friend of the Human Race." He also received the Phoebe Apperson Hearst Award from San Francisco and the St. Francis Xavier Award for Service to Humanity from the Xavier School in Wisconsin in 1971. The St. Francis Assisi award from the City of San Francisco was presented to Father in May 1972 at a civic reception at City Hall. The ceremony then continued at Jones Street with the serving of the 10 millionth meal. Helping Father with the serving that day were Senator Hubert Humphrey, Mayor Alioto and Archbishop McGucken.

In 1977 Alfred received the local (San Francisco)

Jefferson Award, and on June 23, 1977 in Washington D.C. at the Supreme Court—in the presence of Justice Byron (Whizzer) White, Senator John Glenn and Ethel Kennedy among other notables—he received the National Jefferson Award in the category of Greatest Public Service benefiting the local community. Father lost no opportunity to invite the assembled dignitaries to "come and break bread with the poor of the St. Anthony Dining Room." Jacqueline Kennedy Onassis was a member of the board which made the selections for this award.

The Federal Republic of Germany awarded Alfred the Officer's Cross of the Order of Merit First Class in 1954.

He received Honorary Doctorates from the University of San Francisco, St. Mary's College in California, Regis College in Denver and Santa Clara University in California. The University of California, San Francisco, awarded him its President's Award of Merit.

The City again recognized its native son when it dedicated a downtown park as "Father Boeddeker Park." At his funeral in 1994, it was announced that August 7 (Alfred's birthday) would be designated "Father Alfred Boeddeker Day" in San Francisco . . . a fitting tribute to the "patron saint of the Tenderloin." In June 1996, neighbors and friends celebrated the cleanup and reclamation of Boeddeker Park, which had become a hangout for drug dealers and gang members. A Juneteenth party with a baseball game between Tenderloin residents and local police officers was followed by a barbecue. (Juneteenth is a celebration based in the African-American community commemorating June, 1865 when slaves in Texas finally learned they had been freed by the signing of the Emancipation Proclamation in January 1863.)

Alfred was a Knight Commander of the Holy Sepulcher, knighted in Jerusalem in 1977 by the Patriarch of Jerusalem, a rare honor, as well as a Knight of Malta, knighted in San Francisco in 1985. These knighthoods made him Father Sir Alfred Boeddeker, OFM.

The Nobel Peace Prize eluded him, although he was nominated several times by President Ronald Reagan, Senator Dennis DeConcini, Congressman Pete McClosky and Dr. John Walz.

Among the testimonials for the Nobel prize was this from United States Senator Dianne Feinstein, then mayor of San Francisco: " . . . this unsung American who has dedicated his entire life to peace, goodwill and the well-being of all peoples." From Archbishop Quinn: "When first hearing of Alfred as candidate for the Nobel, I was surprised. Knowing him as I do, I'm sure he was embarrassed to know that he—who has never sought publicity—was being considered for so great an honor."

At a family Christmas dinner that same year, he called everyone to attention and said very simply, "I did what I did. I never did any of it for recognition, awards, or prizes."

When the group who organized the effort to get him nominated first met with Alfred to tell him what they would like to do and did he have any objection . . . he was startled. He turned away in embarrassment. "I don't care what you do." Though deeply moved to learn family members cared so much, he left the outcome to God, giving the committee no help or encouragement and providing no materials that might be used to prove his good works. His only comment was, "It is all in God's hands."

Father Alfred's supporters were disappointed that in spite of the nominations, he failed to receive the prize.

People who worked closely with him felt it would have been very difficult for him if he *had* won the Peace Prize. The fame, to be thrust into the spotlight of the news media, would have been hard for such an unassuming man. Yet these same people believed he would have accepted it in good grace, seeing the hand of God in his selection.

Nordahl Grieg, the Norwegian poet who died in a bombing raid over Berlin in World War II, once wrote: "For in creating human dignity, we are creating peace." The committee felt these words were so appropriate to Alfred that it used them as the introduction of the Prize proposal.

When the White House announced that the President had nominated Alfred for the Peace Prize, an invitation to lunch at the White House was issued. Alfred declined, saying he was sorry . . . he was too busy. To a niece he confided, "The invitation was political, and I don't like politics."

OTHER JOBS

In 1948 Father Alfred was charged with the restoration of Mission San Antonio de Padua at Jolon, near King City, California. This mission was almost in total ruins and one of the few missions not surrounded by development. This unique situation made it possible for it to be restored to its original state.

It had a long history. Founded by the Franciscan Friars in 1771, it was once a thriving community. In the 1830s the Mexican government secularized the missions, i.e. the property was taken from the Franciscan missionaries and sold to private landowners. In time this particular piece of land became United States federal property. In 1863 President Abraham Lincoln deeded the Mission property back to the Church and the Franciscans. When William Randolph Hearst of the Hearst Newspapers sold the vast surrounding land to the U.S. Army for taxes in 1939, the Order was able to buy thirty-five more acres from the Army. The area became the Hunter Liggett Military Reservation, generally used for training and maneuvers.

Hearst, whose legendary home San Simeon is just over the coast range hills on the Pacific Ocean, had always been interested in San Antonio and the rest of the missions. The Franciscans had worked since around 1900 to restore the mission. The effort went in spurts. In the 1930s a serious effort was made, but the Second

World War ended that restoration attempt. After the war, the Hearst Foundation gave $500,000 toward the repair and restoration of all twenty-one missions with $50,000 earmarked for San Antonio. This was a start, but, in reality, it provided enough money to buy only some of the thousands of tiles needed.

Alfred, studying at the University of California, was put in charge. He mounted a nationwide drive to collect money. His sister, Josephine, was charged with the mailing and receiving. She enlisted her children and all their school friends. The baby she had a few months later was named Antoinette . . . for the mission.

The blessing of the cornerstone marked the kickoff for the campaign. Father Kenneth Hemiquez, OFM was assigned to take a bell on a nationwide tour. It was not the original bell but one that would hang in the restored church. Among those in attendance that day were Governor—later Chief Justice—Earl Warren, Father Alfred, army officers from Fort Ord in nearby Monterey, and Henry Downie, an historian and authority on California mission restoration. He was to pay close attention to the interior of the church and be the major contractor. In addition there were Spanish dancers, and the Santa Barbara Mission Padre Choristers—composed of around twenty Friars and students—sang. Representatives from the Hollywood film colony included Ann Blythe, Ruth Hussey and Ronald Reagan. Many local people also attended, including a number of Native Americans.

Today Mission San Antonio is first a church with a resident pastor and regular services. It is also open to the public as an historical monument, even though it is a bit off the main highway, U.S. 101.

In 1973 Alfred used his many languages as a translator to the General Chapter of Franciscan Superiors, in Madrid,

Spain. This was a worldwide conference of the Order. He translated German, Spanish and Italian to English. It was said that his Italian was very fine, and German was almost his first language.

He then traveled for nearly two months assisting the Province of the Far East. He could give technical advice and monetary help to its many projects.

Alfred's work was, of course, well known and attracted many people who wished to copy his projects or needed his professional help and expertise. Some examples of California projects are: "The St. Martin de Pobres" food program in the Mission District of San Francisco, serving mainly the local Hispanic population; "The Loaves and Fishes" program in Contra Costa County; "The Knights of Malta Medical Clinic" in the Mexican barrios adjacent to St. Vincent's Hospital in Los Angeles; "St. Elizabeth's Medical Clinic" serving the poor African-American population in Oakland.

Alfred was the United States Prefect for Opus Santorium Angelorium, the Pontifical Commission which, for the last two hundred years, has encouraged study and fostered devotion to the angels. He wrote four books on the subject. He once commented, "Angels are not the cute little cherubs we see on Christmas trees, but the most powerful beings controlling all of God's creation."

Christians, We Are All Priests, which he wrote for his 50th anniversary, was one of his best writings.

A Dominican nun from Christ the King Hermitage remarked, "Alfred was the most spiritual man we have ever known. He saw God's handiwork in DNA, for example. 'Isn't it wonderful that God works in such a way?' He would talk about spirituality and then tell jokes."

ALFRED THE MARIANOLOGIST

Veneration of Mary, the Mother of Jesus, was one of the great devotions of Alfred's life. Father Floyd Lotito remembered that—as a seminarian at the Old Santa Barbara Mission, he first met Alfred in 1954. "We found him very alive with a great love of Mary, and he impressed us with how he served the poor."

Alfred's lifelong dedication led to in-depth study of Mary and her role in the Church. As a canon lawyer, he had a thorough grounding in theology. This led him to become a well-known Marianologist—a theologian who specializes in the truth of the faith in the Blessed Mother . . . her place in the Church, her titles, her place in the life of the faithful and what traditional devotion to Mary has meant through the centuries.

Alfred founded the Franciscan Marian Commission and was its president for a time. He was a member of the International Pontifical Marian Academy. Again he was the moving force and associate editor of the hard cover annual *The Marian Era*, which presented articles by distinguished theologians, especially Americans.

The Marian Center and Library on Golden Gate Avenue was Father's own. When the Franciscan National Marian Congress was held in San Francisco in August 1961, Alfred sponsored a Madonna Festival of sculptures and paintings of Mary. He asked the local Orthodox and Protestant churches to lend their Madonnas.

Many ministers, priests and pastors had Marian images and were willing to share them. The result was that the Festival had icons from Russian, Greek, Armenian, Serbian and Syrian Orthodox groups. The Episcopal Church of St. Mary the Virgin lent an image of Our Lady of Walsingham, England. Alfred's Our Lady of Guadeloupe, the Hope of the Americas, was the center-piece of the Festival. Perhaps the most dramatic icon was the one lent by Mayor George Christopher, pre-sented to him by the Patriarch of Moscow on his visit to Russia.

In 1971 Alfred made it possible for Father Eamon Carroll, Order of Carmelites—then of the Catholic Uni-versity in Washington D.C.—to give a series of lectures on Mary throughout the United States. Father Carroll spoke in almost every state of the Union as well as in Canada. Alfred and Carroll hoped to quiet the fears of many that the Second Vatican Council had somehow lessened Mary's stature in the Church. Alfred's sugges-tions led to the American bishops' joint pastoral letter "Behold Your Mother; Woman of Faith." Carroll was the principal author while Alfred provided ideas and financial support. The text appeared on November 21, 1973, published by the American bishops in English and Spanish and has since been translated into Italian and French. It has received worldwide praise.

In 1987-88 Alfred was the driving force behind a five-day Marian symposium at the University of San Francisco with speakers from many faiths: Orthodox, Lutheran, Anglican, Presbyterian as well as Catholic. He received the Cardinal Wright Award from the Marianlogical Soci-ety of America in 1989, its highest honor.

The Ecumenical Society of the Blessed Virgin Mary, of which Alfred was a member, held an international congress in London, September 1979 for all clergy who believed Mary was the Mother of Christ, the Mother of God. There were ministers of the Methodist church, Episcopal priests as well as priests from the many branches of Orthodoxy. An Episcopal service was held at St. Paul's Cathedral. The clergy from the Church of England joined the group in a Rosary said at Westminster Cathedral, the Roman Catholic Cathedral. A group of some two hundred people, including five Catholic cardinals, were asked to join Father Alfred, a Dominican priest and the Superior of the Benedictines (who would have been the superior of the Abbey were it still Catholic) in the celebration of the Mass in St. Edward the Confessor's Chapel of Westminster Abbey. This was the first Roman Catholic Mass to be celebrated in the Abbey since the Reformation (Edward was the founder of the Abbey and was buried there in January 1066. His death prompted the Norman Conquest of England. Edward was the only English king ever canonized).

Later, Alfred was about to open his Marian Library. The books were bought, shelved and catalogued. Father Carroll was the principal purchasing agent. But now Alfred had no more money. All his normal resources were exhausted, and he had no funds to pay a part-time librarian. The amount needed was $2,400—a pittance compared to the funds he usually dealt with. In his prayers, he told Our Lady it was her library and if she wanted it opened, that amount of money would have to be found. That very afternoon a man stopped by the rectory door, handed an envelope to a brother, who passed it to Alfred just as he was going to supper. After his meal he opened the envelope to find exactly $2,400 in new bills with no indication where the money had come from or why. The library opened, and it had its librarian.

Alfred also had a wonderful collection of statues of the Virgin in the Marian Center. These were gifts from people all around world.

In 1954, in honor of the Marian Year, Father organized a musical presentation at the San Francisco Opera House titled "Mother of All." Two performances were given to a sold-out house. The actor Cameron Mitchell—whose father was a Protestant minister—served as narrator, and Ruth Hussey played Mary.

ALFRED AND THE ARTS

Art and music played a large role in Alfred's life, but these interests were somewhat overshadowed by all his other activities. Yet in the 1950s he started a musical society called the St. Boniface Cultural Society, made up of a group of musicians and artists. It was under the direction of Ernest and Lisa Lonner, German refugees. Some of the music was sacred but most was classical.

He encouraged and financially underwrote the Artists Embassy International founded by Althya Youngman to promote goodwill and understanding through art and music. When Althya met Father Alfred and told him of the work of the organization, he wanted to know if it was truly international. She replied that she had friends who worked with her in England, India, Ceylon and Spain.

"Well, make them officially your representatives. It doesn't matter if they only have a card table for an office. This can be. That's just what we need. Art is like oil in the machinery of humanity."

With that, he gave her a check for $220—which was the exact amount she owed right then for telephone, printing and other bills. She wondered how he could know that was the amount she needed. Later she found out that that morning someone had given Father exactly $220 "to use for God."

Artists Embassy International fostered young artists from all over the world, mostly poor ones. The Children's Art Center, part of Artists Embassy, exchanged the art of children throughout the world. The central idea was peace and love.

San Francisco artist Antonio Sotomeyer was a good friend. He painted a mural of La Madres de los Pobres in the Marian Center of San Francisco, which was later donated to and moved to the chapel in Tijuana. Mary in the mural was seen giving a tortilla to the poor. When the mural was being planned Alfred had a dream that Mary should hold a tortilla but never mentioned it to Sotomeyer. The artist then independently painted in the tortilla. Grace Cathedral commissioned Sotomeyer to do that church's murals, and Alfred—with several other Catholic priests—represented their Church in the dedication of the murals.

One year during the Christmas season, Alfred sponsored a rally in Union Square, the downtown heart of the San Francisco shopping district. The program went for nine evenings with ethnic groups in native dress performing songs and dances of their countries. Alfred attended every performance.

COMMENTS BY FRIENDS

*Overwhelmed is the good part of being challenged.
Status quo—you don't go anywhere. Do what you
always did, and you will get what you always had.*
—Alfred

Hundreds knew and loved Father Alfred and offered tributes to him during his lifetime and after his death. The stories told to this author were, in turn, serious, profound, sad . . . and many very humorous. A sampling follows.

During an interview, Father Floyd remembered, "He loved his family. He traced it from the Gelhauses' arrival in America around 1875 into the many branches. He gathered the names and addresses of around 800 relatives and showed their relationships to each other. Family reunions on the Farm would draw from 250-300 people.

"He was good to his family, yet could be very hard on nieces and nephews from time to time. And his family did for him. Some were very successful and gave large sums to the Foundation. His brothers worked for him—sometimes for pay, often without.

"Yes, there were warts on the man. If not, he wouldn't be human. If he didn't have warts, there would be no merit—no glory."

A Father O'Malley sent a taped greeting for a reception: "If the lives of men were to be measured by one standard, it would be to the extent to which they have fostered understanding and awareness of the need of others. By that standard, I salute you." Some in the audience immediately recognized the voice. Father O'Malley was in the movie *Going My Way*. He was perhaps better known as Bing Crosby.

Father Floyd also commented on the many years that he worked with Father, "Alfred is a man who as a friend leaves you with all your freedom intact. He doesn't try to make someone follow his style or his way. He allows people the freedom to be themselves . . . to grow and respond as they see the way. It is a great gift which only big people can confer."

Alfred's good friend, the former mayor of San Francisco, George Christopher once stated: "The most indelible impression was conveyed (to me) by a Catholic priest who was embarking (1950) on an ancient yet newly molded custom—feeding the hungry. His tall frame—his convincing, almost tearful eyes—his warm and friendly approach—his manifest compassion and deep-rooted sense of charity and concern for the less fortunate, all seemed to permeate the total atmosphere when Father Alfred entered the room. He didn't have to say very much, for his sincerity was so evident."

Bishop Mark Hurley called Alfred "a politician's dream . . . he feeds the hungry, provides them with medical care, then with housing, and finally rehabilitation at no cost to the public treasury. How wonderful for a city. Alfred is a man devoted to life. He believes in life. He is the antithesis of the idea that a life is worthless. There is no man, no woman, no child who is not a human being. They may be down but they are never out. What he touches is transformed, for he is a man of genius, but also imagination and a man of prayer."

Rabbi Joseph Asher of Temple Emanu-El, and chaplain of the San Francisco Police Force, was a good friend of Alfred's and said the following in a prayer at a civic reception honoring him: "One of Your favorite sons, friend of the poor, shepherd to the forgotten, whose labors fulfill Thy highest mandate; always of good cheer. He radiates faith and confidence—and all of us bask in their warmth. May God's grace continue to envelop him, preserve him in health and vigor. Alfred personifies the best of Your creation and we are enriched by him. As we break bread together, may we be nourished in body and in spirit as he nurtures tens of thousands with substance and with love."

Archbishop Quinn said, "All you have done, you have done in loving fidelity to the Church and the Franciscans. In a society that does not care for the less fortunate, you cared. Not with flamboyance do you care but with humility bolstered by your faith in your God that what you are doing and have been doing is the Lord's work."

Father Giles, who was close to Alfred for many years, recalled, "He was a tremendously spiritual person with the awareness of God at all times. He read a tremendous number of spiritual books . . . reading, rereading, absorbing the ideas and working them out for himself."

Father Floyd described how, once on Holy Thursday, Alfred asked him to bring him communion. "He seemed to glow with faith. I never saw anything like it."

ALFRED ANECDOTES

I have not met his equal in kindness, compassion and selfless devotion to the welfare of every living creature since he left this mortal world to assume his rightful place in the deified seat he occupies today. I pray that his benevolent spirit may guide our troubled world today.

—George Christopher

Dr. Leach of the San Franciscan Council of Churches commented, "He radiates such joy and warmth that when you see him, you have to smile. Alfred has the angels going for him."

Alfred loved to tell stories. He was famous for his jokes, which often had a serious undercurrent. People loved to tell stories about him. A few are collected here.

Alfred was regarded as a saint in his hometown, a man who could do the impossible. But when he tried to purchase an apartment house near St. Boniface Church, he was stymied. Vincent Hallinan did not want to sell. Hallinan, a legend in the Bay Area, was a famous lawyer and a former Catholic, now an avowed atheist. He had made headlines when he once sued the Catholic Church to prove the existence of hell. Alfred's only response to the frustration of not acquiring the Hallinan property was a gentle smile and a soft, "Give the devil his due."

At a family party in San Francisco in the mid-1970s, Alfred was introduced to George Belcher, a wealthy developer, who said, "Father you are doing a wonderful work. I have you in my will."

"Great," said the hostess, "George has money running out of his ears, Father."

"George, let's see your ears. No, you are wrong, George doesn't have money running out of his ears."

Directly in back of St. Boniface's stood a venerable institution, the President Follies, a burlesque house. Father and "the girls" greeted each other very cordially when their paths crossed on the street, but one of the strippers had a disconcerting habit of coming to the church and "flashing." One day the woman dropped her coat and stood in the middle of St. Boniface Church in the buff. When Alfred saw her, he told the sacristan to throw the benediction robe over her. The sacristan saw this as an improper use of the sacred cloak. Alfred insisted, "I'm the pastor, and I say put the robe on her." It was, and she was quickly removed from the church.

Another problem was the location of the Follies. The loud music from the 2AM show was a bit of a distraction when the friars were trying to sleep. However, the property fitted in very nicely with the expansion needs of the church. Alfred got his brother Joe, a real estate broker, to buy it. Everything was done through third parties; otherwise the sale might be jeopardized. Things went smoothly; the property was purchased, and Father Alfred became the proprietor of the largest burlesque house west of Chicago . . . for a short time. As one of his first acts of ownership, Father sprinkled the building with Holy Water. Apparently he also acquired the costumes. What was done with those, no one remembers. The family referred to this venture as "Big

Al's Burlesque House." The property was later taken over by Catholic Charities and now is the site of the Dorothy Day Center, an affordable housing complex for seniors.

The Living Crib was a tradition of the Christmas celebrations at St. Boniface. Father had the idea of life-sized figures and live animals. John Korbus, his maintenance man, and Frank Schepergerdes went to Petaluma and obtained a few sheep. These were displayed with the life-sized statues. Sometimes, to create greater interest, men from the line volunteered to dress in costume and stand very still in the tableau. When they finally moved, it would be a great surprise to the onlookers. The children particularly loved it. People who worked for the Foundation and the Church remember that by Epiphany in January, the whole thing got quite fragrant with a ripe barnyard smell.

In those days the inner courtyard was not fenced off nor locked in the evenings. One night some street people climbed down to the living crib. They killed the sheep and dressed them out, built a fire over which they roasted part of the living crib. That was the end of that!

Frank tells of taking a cow and a calf downtown to Union Square for a media event publicizing Spreckels Russell Creamery, which had done so much for the Dining Room by donating milk, butter, ice cream and cheese. Father felt he owed them one. The cow and the calf had on blankets proclaiming that they were from the Spreckels Creamery: "This is the cow that gives milk to the Dining Room." It got the Dining Room and Spreckels a good deal of attention, as well as Frank's close attention to cleaning the street!

On his weekly visits to the Farm, Father loved to eat with the family and enjoyed Greta's good German cooking. Often she baked raisin bread. Now, the kids could all speak German so Alfred coined a word ... *Fliegenbrot* ... fly bread. He solemnly told the children that the dots were flies from the barn that he had just caught and stuffed into the slices. Frank and Greta's kids were too smart for that one, but everyone loved the joke, and it stayed a bond between the children and Alfred as long as he lived.

Some of the humorous stories about the man were not just confined to the United States. Once after a conference in Rome, Alfred was traveling by rail to Cologne, Germany, and the compartment became very warm. Alfred tried and tried to open the window. Suddenly the train stopped. Excited voices shouted throughout the train: "Somebody must have pulled the emergency brake!" This frightened Alfred. He had no idea what the penalty for such a transgression was, so he quickly changed compartments. The train started up again. No one suspected a man in a Franciscan robe of such a "crime."

If things weren't moving along fast enough, Alfred often would set an example. These examples did not always turn out well.

Once his crew was painting the Madonna Residence for the bishop's visit the next day. The work was not moving quickly enough to suit Father. He decided to help.

"John, is there any paint? I want to help."

"On top of the closet and the brush is on the floor."

So Alfred reached for the paint but there was no lid on the can and the whole thing went down the front of Alfred, all over his one and only robe. So the crew—and particularly his secretary Beth Payne—spent the whole afternoon cleaning him up. He smelled of paint for days and days. But the Residence was freshly painted for the bishop's blessing, and everyone went home with a hilarious story at Father's expense.

A retired professional woman, who found herself in greatly reduced circumstances, had the responsibility of an 89-year-old mother thrust upon her. Alfred talked to her very seriously about "getting out, doing something for yourself, don't let this take over your whole life." On the way home she realized Father must be remembering his beloved sister, Louise. He often characterized her "the smartest one of all of us." Lou had cared for their mother and had done just what he was warning against. She never recovered physically or emotionally and was never really able to function again after her mother's death. The woman wrote Alfred a quick note: "Don't worry, I'm no Lou. I'm tougher than that." The next time Alfred saw her, he simply took her hand. "I got your letter. Good." (Yes, she *did* survive the long illness of her mother.)

Good friends from Hillsborough sent their new Rolls Royce to pick up Alfred, who—in his patched and stained Franciscan robe—settled into the back seat and admired the auto. "This is a very nice car. Is it expensive?"

The astonished chauffeur, in livery, could only reply, "Yes, very expensive."

The next day, when Alfred found out *how* expensive, he declared, "I could build four churches for that money."

One example of his great kindness is the story of Bill: a brilliant man, a fine person, a dedicated teacher, a great coach and a gentleman. He was the head basketball coach at the high school where he also taught science and math. He would then drive home and coach the basketball team of the local Catholic high school. Bill's wife and children were all Catholic, but he had never been baptized. In his late fifties he suffered a massive heart attack and seemed on the road to recovery when he had another attack. On his way into surgery, he asked his wife to baptize him. He did not make it. When Alfred heard the story, he said, "What a good man. His was a baptism of desire. He certainly was saved even without the last minute rites." Bill's widow treasured the letter she received from Alfred above all others.

The extended family, which had been very close in the years after immigration, in time became scattered. "We seem to meet at weddings and funerals," was the common remark. At Bertha's funeral, Henry Gelhaus, her nephew, came. He had lived with the Boeddeker family when he was an apprentice at Union Iron Works. In 1949, Henry was the West Coast manager of Todd Shipyards, close to the end of a distinguished career. He had not seen Alfred in many years, and remarked to another cousin, "No, he is not going to get any money out of me, Frank. He can ask all he wants but no—not a dime." Frank just smiled. When Henry's car came to pick him up, he said, "It has been good to see all of you even if the occasion was not a happy one. We have to get together more. Oh, by the way, Father, can I see you in the kitchen?"

Both men came back into the living room smiling, Henry putting his pen back in his jacket pocket.

Frank laughed. "Not going to get a dime out of *me*, huh, Henry?"

"Shut up, Frank. He never asked." And he never did.

The Chief of Police of the City of San Francisco, a good friend, was in Alfred's office telling him he was a wonderful person but a poor judge of character. Alfred had just sent a man with a very tough reputation to the bank with a large amount of cash.

"You made a mistake. The guy will take off. You'll never see your money or him again." At that moment the man appeared with a bank receipt for the full amount.

Alfred loved to tell jokes. One such was of a police officer stopping a man with a penguin in his car. The officer suggested that the man take the bird to the zoo, a better place for it. The next week that officer saw the same man and the penguin. "I thought you were going to take the bird to the zoo?" / "Oh, I did and he liked it so much, I'm going to take him to Disneyland."

Actually that was just a warm-up for a more important story. A battered violin had received a top bid of only $3 at an auction. Then someone wiped it clean and started to play "as sweet as angels sing." The bid went to $3000! When people asked what had changed its worth, "The touch of a Master's hand" was the reply. Alfred would smile and continue, "And many a person with life out of tune, and battered and torn with sin, is auctioned cheap to a thoughtless crowd, much like the old violin. A mess of pottage, a glass of wine, a game, and they travel on, they're going once, and going twice and they're going—and almost gone. But the Master comes and the foolish crowd never can quite understand the worth of a soul, and the change that is wrought, by the touch of the Master's hand."

Frank Schepergerdes tells another story: "One day we sat in Alfred's office with the Chief of Police, who did much for him and Alfred said, 'Gee, you know, I've got this building to go up, and I need a storage building to store a few things. I don't have any lumber at all.'

"'Father, I've got that all fixed. I can get all the lumber you want.'

"'You can? What a good thing.'

"'I'll tell you what. Right after midnight, you meet me at the back gate of Goodman's Lumber Company. You and I will load up the truck. Frank can drive.'

"'Oh, wouldn't that make the headlines—the Chief of Police and Father Alfred robbing the Goodman yard. I'm afraid that won't work.'"

In the late 1930s, a gentleman came to the Old Santa Barbara Mission and asked Alfred to show him around, which he gladly did. The church, the grounds, the Sacred Garden, everything. Would he like to see more of Santa Barbara? Yes, he would.

Alfred got out the friars' old car and drove to Montecito where the great estates of the city were located. Father knew most of the people, so he was allowed to show his guest the gardens, including the famous Lotus Garden of Rare Plants. Finally the two men got back to the Old Mission.

"This is a terrible car you are driving around. Is this the best you have?"

Alfred explained that the Order was poor, and they were trying to keep the thing running.

"I'll send you a car."

Months went by, and the entire incident had been forgotten when the door bell of the Friary rang. A call for Father Alfred. At the curb stood a large, yellow Studebaker convertible.

"This was sent for the Order and Father Alfred to show people around and to use for your business."

The gentleman turned out to be the president of Studebaker Motors. Later the yellow convertible went to Oakland where Father drove it to the University of California in Berkeley while attending classes there. Much later it was sent to the nuns in Mexico. Brother

Frank says with a smile, "It was the kind of thing that went on all the time with Alfred."

What do you give a Franciscan who has taken a vow of poverty? It was always a problem for Alfred's friends and family. Since Alfred smoked, that seemed a perfect answer. This was in the 1930s before people were aware of the health risks. One Christmas he received so many cartons of cigarettes, there was a very large stack of them in his cell. When Alfred saw them, he considered his habit, then went to his superior and told him to give them all away. "I'll keep them for you till you change your mind."

"No, give them away. I will never smoke again." He never did.

George Christopher, owner of Christopher Dairies, remembers Alfred coming to his office and saying, "George, guess why I am here?"

"I always reminded him that I could guess why because my cows were working overtime to supply him with the free milk he needed for the Dining Room. And always, as he apologized for his regular request, I would always reassure him that my benevolent and generous cows were happy that their product was going to a worthy humanitarian cause." Once though, Christopher asked him to offer a special prayer for the cows, to suggest that for a change, they offer a small supply of bourbon instead of milk. Alfred laughed joyfully and said that the decision rested with a "higher authority."

Alfred visited Jerusalem shortly after that city was reunited following the Six Days War in the Middle East. He and a group of friends went to the Church of the Mount of Olives. The others wanted to continue on to somewhere else, but Alfred could see their hotel across a valley and said he wished to go back to rest. It was just a short walk across an open field. On the other side of the valley, a very startled soldier asked, "Where did you come from?"

"Oh, I walked across that valley."

"My God, man. That field is completely mined!"

Alfred decided his guardian angel had protected him again.

THE END

A visionary and a doer of deeds.
—Sister Michael of the Hermitage,
speaking of Alfred

Alfred had a stroke in 1991. Nuns who visited him told how he tried to laugh when he could not talk. His speech returned, but he was confined to a wheelchair for the last few years of his life. But he went right on working . . . planning for the Year 2000, sending out rosaries, organizing the work of La Madre de los Pobres and the Sacred Heart Society, seeing people, hearing confessions, saying Mass.

Then, late in 1993, a small notice appeared in Herb Caen's column that Father Alfred was back in the hospital and not doing well. A niece called Alfred and wanted to know why he had not let the family know. "Oh," he answered, "I didn't want to worry anyone."

There were many, many visitors, among them his old friend Dr. Curry, who remembers their last long talk . . . "We settled the problems of the world. Then I said to him, 'You are not long for this world.' His reply was a soft, 'I'm ready.' I said, 'God be with you.' That was the last time I saw him."

Alfred passed away quietly on January 1, 1994, while hearing the confession of a relative, doing his priestly duties to the very end. He often said that the day of his death would be the happiest day of his life; he would see his God, whom he had served so nobly for ninety years.

The news of his passing was carried on the wire services nationwide. He lay in state for a day. The funeral was a very public one. The police placed honor guards inside the church, and mounted officers were posted before the church. The funeral itself was attended by more than 1000 people: city, state and national leaders such as the mayor, members of Congress, representatives from many religious groups, family, many friends and his beloved poor.

The funeral was not sorrowful. The Mass of Resurrection was a joyous service—the celebration of a great man's wonderful life. A niece observed, "It was as if we were all standing at the gates of heaven watching Father enter."

Of course, there was a typical Alfred incident. San Francisco Mayor Frank Jordan was in the first seat of the first pew on the left of the church, which was reserved for dignitaries. Seated next to him was an aide who was called away before the service started. A ragged guest and friend of Alfred's came to the front of the church and knelt by the coffin, which he lovingly touched. People in the front row saw his lips moving as if talking to Father. When the man stood, he saw the empty seat next to the Mayor and went over and sat down. Family members who watched it all said, "Alfred told him where to find a seat."

Typical of Father's life and the people he touched, a handsome man in his mid-forties dressed in very expensive casual clothes—tears streaming down his face—sat next to a man, silent in his grief, with cardboard wrapped around his feet for shoes. Behind the two, a man whispered, No, he was not taking communion. "I am an Episcopal priest."

It was said of Alfred that he was a man of continual light and tremendous kindness. "To start something like this, he must have been a person of deep compassion and real conviction," said a guest who declined to give his name. One person made the telling comment that working with the poor was not glamorous. It was hard work.

A 55-year-old woman who did not want to be identified admitted, "I fell through the cracks, and without Father Boeddeker there wouldn't be a catcher. He was a sweet man. He was nothing but love. He gave me a talking-to about five weeks ago. He was advising me not to give up; to stand up and fight and don't forget to ask for help when you need it."

Crosby Walker, a patron of the Dining Room on and off since the mid-'70s, said, "He was a gentle giant. You'd see him around here in the neighborhood, if not in the dining hall, and he was always smiling. He never made you feel like less than he was. He'd stop and talk regardless of how low you might seem to be to yourself." Walker was a Korean war veteran who had trouble returning to civilian life and "turned to the bottle for consolation."

"Granny" Brooks had been attending St. Boniface Church for more than sixty years. "I don't think I will be able to go eat at the Dining Room for a while; for now I've lost my appetite."

The thoughts of many of the Dining Room patrons were that: "Alfred not only saved my soul, he saved me from having a doomed life."

Jeanne Zarka Brooks, Executive Director of the St. Anthony Foundation, said, "That guy was absolutely, to the day he died, hopeful about the power of love. His advice to me was: 'Just thank people; never worry about where the money comes from. People are generous.'"

Robert Lentz, a well-known icon artist, painted the Madonna icon which now hangs directly over the door in St. Boniface Church. It is called *The Mother of the Streets* and shows a black madonna. A copy was printed on the cover of Alfred's funeral brochure.

He was buried at the Old Mission in Santa Barbara with his brother Franciscans.

Young Dustin Hartmann had met Father on several occasions. The child was shown Alfred's obituary with the comment that, "You will meet many people in your life: rich, poor, good, bad—"

"But I will never meet a greater man," interrupted the ten-year-old.

From the Rule of St. Francis which was read at Alfred's funeral:

"Let all the Friars be clad in poor garments. May they patch them with sackcloth and other pieces with the blessing of God. I warn and exhort them not to despise or judge those they see clad in soft and colorful apparel and using choice food or drink. But rather let each one judge himself.

"I counsel and warn and exhort my Friars in the Lord Jesus Christ that when they are abroad they neither dispute, content in words nor judge others but show themselves peaceful and modest, mild and humble, speaking modestly to all as is becoming."

HONORS

Among the many honors Father Alfred received were:

- Officers' Cross of the Order of Merit of the Federal Republic of Germany, 1955.

- National Jefferson Award for "Greatest Public Service Benefiting a Local Community," presented by the American Institute for Public Service in Washington, D.C., June 23, 1977.

- City of San Francisco Jefferson Award by the *San Francisco Examiner*, 1977.

- St. Francis of Assisi Award by the City of San Francisco, 1972.

- Phoebe Apperson Hearst Award, for one of the City's most Distinguished Ten, *San Francisco Examiner*, 1974.

- Honorary Degrees
  - ‡ University of San Francisco, 1972, Doctor of Public Service.
  - ‡ St. Mary's College, Moraga, California, 1978, Doctor of Humane Letters.
  - ‡ Regis College, Denver, Colorado, 1982, Doctor of Humanities.
  - ‡ University of Santa Clara, Santa Clara, California, 1984, Doctor of Public Service.

‡President's Award of Merit, University of California, San Francisco, 1986.

- St. Francis Xavier Award for Service to Humanity by Xavier High School, Manitowoc, Wisconsin, 1979.

- Installed as Knight of the Holy Sepulcher in Jerusalem, September 14, 1977.

- Installed as a Knight Commander of the Holy Sepulcher.

- Installed as a Knight of Malta.

- St. Ignatius College, President's Award as Friend of the Human Race.

- Laura Bride Powers Award for contribution to the City of San Francisco.

- Pro-Life Award from United For Life Organization.

- The Cardinal Wright Award from the Marianological Society of America, 1989

- Boeddeker Park named in his honor, San Francisco.

- Resolutions of recognition from various governors, Senators and Assemblymen, and members of the Board of Supervisors for the City and County of San Francisco.

- Telegrams of congratulation from Presidents Kennedy, Nixon, Carter, Reagan.

- Resolution by San Francisco Board of Supervisors, "Father Alfred Day" August 7, his birthday.

ACTIVITIES

- 1928–1930 Assistant Pastor, Old Mission, Santa Barbara, California
- Pastor St. Rafael Church, Goleta, California
- Chaplain, General Hospital, Santa Barbara
- 1933–1948 Professor at Franciscan Theologate, Santa Barbara
- Dean of Studies, in charge of Houses of Study on Pacific Coast
- Founder and Director of St. Mary's Center, Santa Barbara
- 1946–49 Member of Franciscan Provincial Council
- 1949–81 Pastor of St. Boniface Church, San Francisco, California
- Director at various times:
  - ‡ Parish Executive Committee
  - ‡ Altar Society
  - ‡ St. Vincent De Paul Society
  - ‡ St. Anthony's Helpers
  - ‡ Pious Union of St. Joseph
  - ‡ Pious Union of St. Anthony
  - ‡ St. Boniface Choir

‡St. Boniface Arts Center

‡Founder of Serra Center and Library.

‡Marian Center and Library

‡Catholic Friendship Club (for adults over 40)

- Established St. Boniface Credit Union and St. Francis Family Guild.

- Organized National Franciscan Marian Congress, 1954.

- Diocesan Director of Franciscan Missionaries of Mary and their Confessor.

- Confessor to Sisters of St. Joseph (Chinese Mission).

- Confessor to BVM (St. Brigid's Parish).

- Confessor to Daughters of St. Paul, San Francisco.

- Confessor to Dominican Sisters (St. Anthony's Parish).

- Guardian at St. Boniface; vicar and discreet at other times.

- Dean of Archdiocese

- President:
    ‡Franciscan Marian Commission of the United States

    ‡San Francisco Chapter of "People to People"

    ‡International Envoys Club

    ‡Western Branch of Marianological Society of America

    ‡Artists Embassy International

    ‡Sacred Heart Society

    ‡Logan Fellowship

    ‡La Madre de los Pobres

- Cofounder and Director: Missionary Sisters of the Queen of Peace, Mexico.

- Member of the Board of Directors:

  ‡ Pontifical International Marian Academy (Rome).

  ‡ Friends of Korean Orphans.

  ‡ Pan-Africa House, San Francisco.

  ‡ Project Concern, for blind children.

- Member:

  ‡ The Governor's Committee for Aging.

  ‡ Marianological Society of America.

- Organized and built (or assisted):

  ‡ Helped in the building of eleven houses in Mexico for Missionary Sisters, including Ciudad de Misericordia.

  ‡ Poor Clares Monastery, Aptos, California.

  ‡ Restoration of Mission San Antonio de Padua, Jolon, California.

  ‡ Church in Bad Herzfeld, Germany.

  ‡ Churches in Mexico: Tijuana, Ensenada, Leon, Mexico City.

  ‡ Chapels in Tijuana and Nogales, Mexico and Petaluma, California.

  ‡ Villa Nazareth in Higuey, Dominican Republic: 70 homes for low-income people.

  ‡ Outpatient treatment clinic for lepers in Managua, Nicaragua and Darios Medical projects in Ecuador, rural immunization program and rural medical center.

‡ Housing in Haiti (provided money).

‡ Kerela, India for small homes (provided money).

- Promoted Mass stipends for bishops in South America, Africa and Asia.

- Chairman and Associate Editor, *The Marian Era.*

- Published *Second Spring* magazine for the elderly.

- Published *Spiral,* a devotional newsletter.

These words of faith were found in a notebook written by Alfred and printed in celebration of his seventy years as a Franciscan Friar on August 1, 1991.

I will never speak ill of anyone in the slightest.
Detach your heart from the things of the world and consider that there is nothing else in this world except you and God alone.
Don't speak of the vanities of the world; desire to speak only of Him.
He who loves purity, not only diligently banishes all impure fancies, but does so with horror and abomination.
And, in the same way, he who really loves humility, far from taking pleasure in praise and honor is displeased by them, and instead of fleeing from humiliations, embraces them.
Glorify God by giving Him credit for all the good He does through you.
Humility always—He gets the praise.
He must increase—you decrease.
Surrender to God, and He will do everything for you.
Turn away from evil, learn to do God's will;
The Lord will strengthen you if you obey Him.
God of Mercy and Love,
Help us to follow the example of Mary.
Always ready to do Your will, at the message of an angel,
She welcomed Your eternal Son, and, filled with the light
Of Your Spirit, she became the temple of Your Word.

This lengthier piece was also found:

I am a poem of God

I.

A poem gives existence to nothing; it is the music of thought, it reveals the loveliness of nature, it is the utterance of deep and heartfelt truth, it is love's chosen apostle.

I am the poem of the love of God; the Creator stamped His image forcibly on me, as on a page; the spirit of beauty then sprang up in the footsteps of His going, and upon nothingness and darkness, a sunlit bank empurpled with blossoms of life, appeared. Truly I am a poem, a thing of God.

As a Christian, I am the noblest poem of God; I continually reveal those magnificent types of beauty and truth which God has set in the soul of a Christian.

I am a poem, the creation of God's ceaseless thought. My life comes from His breath eternally drawn in love. From His loving thought I was born; it ever sustains me, doling out existence and life to me each moment; from it I continually grow, work, pray and sleep. All this is the fruit of His one ineffable creative thought, which is forever alive in me.

"O the depth of the riches and wisdom and the knowledge of God."

II.

In this one thought of God is contained from all eternity the picturesque and delightful landscape, the huge glaciers in their superb whiteness, the vast ocean, the countless, jewel-like stars, those myriads of infinitely minute insects, the shape of the lilies of the fields, the flowers of the valley, and each strand of mass. —By this one, simple eternal, immutable and loving Thought, all things and all events, past present and to be are created and re-created each second.

Never will any person, not even the greatest human genius, give life to anything by his mere thought. Yet the whole world and I myself are the crystallization of God's one thought . . . a magnificent moving drama, with God as its author.

Well should my poem of love break into song, for music calls on the spirit, and my poem resembles music, another of God's most magnificent presents. With lyre and harp, I join the harmonious voice of all creation, and like the echo of the invisible world, I sing,

"O mighty, wonderful God!
I praise you, supreme and incomparable
Thought, eternally real and fruitful!"

III.

But this Thought—what or who is it? In the Blessed Trinity, the Word is the expression of all that is of the Father, and of all possible creation. From eternity, always and even now, the Father has thought one eternal thought; it is a loving thought. Into it He emptied and expressed the depths of His own infinite being and all creatures. What he expressed, what He generated or gave birth to, was and is the Word. So, in the Word, in the Second Person of the august Trinity, is to be found that infinite thought which contains the nature of the Father and the ideas which from the make-up and the events of all creatures; rocks, stars, flowers, animals, man. The Word is their prototype, and He is their source, for all things proceed from God through the Word. Each creature realizes or brings out the Word, this one thought which is, as it were, fractured into trillions. Each creature in its own individual nature corresponds to this divine idea; it manifests the complete Word in its own way. Each has intimate relations with the Word; and its individual holiness consists in carrying into effect the particular thought (plan) as God conceived of it before its creation, when during eternity it exists as a distinct idea in the Word.

Well may I sing as I compose and express this thought. Through it may my poem, filled with music divine, delight the ear, recreate the mind, and fill the heart . . .

"In the beginning was the Word . . .
and the Word was God!
The Word was made flesh . . .
and dwelt among us."

If I do not express His thought, the idea He wants me to be and to live, His thought and plan for me will never be expressed. For nothing is like me. God never duplicates anything in His world, from fingerprints to the individual tree leaves. He doesn't want exact copies. No one can be another St. Francis. Each person in his thought, words and deeds is expected to express the eternal Word according to a picked and individualized idea or plan.

Like the Word Himself, my expression of Word should be pure and perfect. What impairs this pure expression is my discord with the Divine idea, which is manifested in each moment and event. I respect His idea in preferring my own contrary ideas. Through my sins, infidelities, resistance to His inspirations, through views that are entirely of this world. These acts of mine spoil and disfigure the divine idea in me.

What results from this is that there is not a clear mirror of the Word's infinite beauty, but a badly tarnished one. My mysterious free will has withstood His thought, it has betrayed the divine Artist's sculpturing fingers. If I would stop this ill-use of my free will, His long-suffering goodness would set about restoring and refashioning the image of the word in me. So, with Mary, I plead,

"Behold the handmaid of the Lord.

Be it done to me

According to Your Word."

The writer of my poem of love is the Holy Spirit of love; He is the "finger of God's right hand." This Spirit of Christ will write His gospel of love in me; each act will express in me Christ's Word in a lovely poem. The paper is the soul; my actions, including sufferings, are the ink.

He will write a beautiful poem; and not a day will pass in which the type will not be set, the ink applied, and the sheets of verses printed. But we humans, here on earth, are in the night of faith; the paper is blacker than the ink, the characters are confused; the language is of another world. We cannot understand it, so my poem can only be read on the last day, when it will be drawn from the press of this life and published. It will be read only in heaven.

"Come, Holy Spirit.

Come from the Father

and glorify Christ

by forming Him in me. Alleluja!"

The Three Divine Persons are delighted with the Poem of love that is forming. They see that every line is vibrant, like the notes in a symphony; for they hear the Word's sweetest sounds flowing out clearest, as I express him in the musical language of divine praise.

Like King David, the soul is filled with joy; it chants and sings in its sanctuary of God's love. Songs exalting the Word come from its lips as companions of the verses. The soul, like Mary, breaks out in praising the Word, Who lives within it. For God has set up another tabernacle; in this tabernacle is the Host, in which the Word hides.

I am the living Poem of the love of Jesus, the Word, being
written daily, syllable by syllable, by His own Holy Spirit,
to the praise of the God of Immense Majesty.
"Mighty and wonderful are Your works,
Lord, God Almighty:
May the Father, the Word, and the Holy Spirit
be praised forever. Alleluja!"
— Fr. Alfred, OFM

In an editorial for *Adult Information Digest* of October/
November 1993, shortly before his death, Father wrote
eloquently:

Many important things, because they are ordinary, are
taken for granted. We fail to appreciate them. Reflecting
on their value would make us enjoy them far more. Simple,
wonderful things are constantly satisfying the hungers of
the body and readily absorbed sights and sounds ease the
yearnings of the mind and soul.

Take that very essential yet common need of our life, water, one of God's greatest creatures, the only one familiar
to us in all three forms, liquid, solid and gas.

Water is so "humble" as Francis of Assisi would say, yet
its universal importance overwhelms us. Clearly in view,
we see it in the clouds, rain, dew, fog, and ice, in the riv-
ers, lakes and oceans. Unseen, it exists almost everywhere.
It has been called "the blood of the soil," "the husband of
the seed," "the father of all plants"; even great redwoods
are its children.

The versatility of water is almost infinite, conferring its
benefactions on countless creatures on every square mile
of land and sea. It never can sleep, knows no rest and
never dies. It is majestic in its strength, unlimited in its

power, indestructible even in fire. Its authority is absolute: it turns turbines, moves locomotives and ships. It is the most common component of the living body, actually its essential major ingredient, indispensable in practically every human endeavor.

When we think of it, our body is 70 percent water, which is one-third in the blood and other body fluids, and the remaining two-thirds in the billions of tiny cells that make up living tissue; water constitutes 75 percent of our muscles, even 22 percent of our bones. Do we appreciate the essential value of the common drop of water?

There are many other common things which we need and use every day and yet seem to take for granted, such as our five sense organs: eyes, ears, nose, mouth and hands. We use these not only to satisfy the daily yearning of our sensitive nature, our body and its feelings, but also to deliver food to the imagination. In fact our senses supply material for the mind, because "nothing is in the mind that wasn't in one of the senses."

These "ordinary senses" fill big gaps in our lives. They absorb all of Nature's beautiful traits, its grace and the fine touch of its harmony and perfection. In doing, they weave sublime feelings and ideas into our souls.

What a joy for our sense of sight to watch a meadow lark in festive garb soaring into the heavens, or an eagle swimming the heights of the sky. They stir our own longings to rise and soar aloft, to emancipate the soul by the love of something higher, and not to be depressed, not to let tormenting worries ground us.

This ability to draw good from all of God's creatures reveals that there is within us a mysterious ingredient, a kind of positive electricity. Often it is not appreciated, usually taken for granted. It gives us ability to lift ourselves up through such common things as the sunshine, the forest, the ocean, the brook, the meadow, a flower, a healing wayside.

That ability was deeply rooted in Francis of Assisi. He could contemplate and value these everyday things of life, every drop of water, the air, the plants and flowers, the stars, Brother Sun and Sister Moon, because each is a marvelous revelation and gift of God. Through these creatures, God's goodness and beauty peep forth. They have been given to fill us with an overflowing measure of life, cordiality, consolation and joy. Their innate perfections relax our inner tensions and help us to overlook the faults and imperfections of persons who frequently are stumbling-blocks to others and who by offensive manners tend to be a dead-weight upon the souls of those whom they trouble.

An exciting experience—possibly even a renaissance of a personal transfiguration—can take place when a person becomes fully aware of the ordinary things in life. Then when one drinks of the "common" water, it will turn into the bubbling "living waters" of spiritual truth, satisfying both mind and heart.

—Alfred Boeddeker, OFM

ADDRESSES

St. Anthony Foundation
121 Golden Gate Avenue
San Francisco, CA 94102

St. Anthony Farms
11205 Valley Ford Road
Petaluma, CA 94952

Madonna Residence
1055 Pine Street
San Francisco, CA 94109

The Hermitage of Christ the King
6501 Orchard Station Road
Sebastopol, CA 95472

Casa de los Pobres
P.O. Box 432256
San Ysidro, CA 92143-2256

La Madre de los Pobres
121 Golden Gate Avenue
San Francisco, CA 94102